CURRENT BUDGETING PRACTICES IN U.S. INDUSTRY

Recent Titles from Quorum Books

CURRENT BUDGETING PRACTICES IN U.S. INDUSTRY

The State of the Art

Srinivasan Umapathy

Foreword by John Leslie Livingstone

Quorum Books
New York • Westport, Connecticut • London

Library of Congress Cataloging-in-Publication Data

Umapathy, Srinivasan.
  Current budgeting practices in U.S. industry.

  Bibliography: p.
  Includes index.
  1. Budget in business. 2. Corporations—
United States—Finance—Planning. I. Title.
HG4028.B8U46 1987   658.1'54   87-5969
ISBN 0-89930-250-5 (lib. bdg. : alk. paper)

British Library Cataloguing in Publication Data is available.

Library of Congress Catalog Card Number: 87-5969
ISBN: 0-89930-250-5

First published in 1987 by Quorum Books

Greenwood Press, Inc.
88 Post Road West, Westport, Connecticut 06881

Printed in the United States of America

∞

The paper used in this book complies with the
Permanent Paper Standard issued by the National
Information Standards Organization (Z39.48-1984).

10 9 8 7 6 5 4 3 2 1

I dedicate this book
with love, affection, and gratitude
to my parents,
Kuttalam Rajagopalan Srinivasan
and Rajalakshmi Srinivasan.

Contents

List of Tables

Chapter 6. Budget Manager Characteristics

Foreword

It is an honor to write a foreword for a book authored by a friend and colleague whom I very much admire. But the honor is all the more when the book is so truly outstanding. I do believe that this book is a landmark study and that it will soon be recognized as a classic.

How does one justify such high praise? My reasons are strong and clear. First, based on sound research, the book offers definitive steps to make budgeting effective in any company. These steps can also help to improve the processes of long-range planning, management motivation, performance evaluation, and strategy implementation, through linking these processes with effective budget practices. As the author states: "Budgeting is like a surgeon's knife. In . . . skilled hands . . . it can save . . . life. However, in the hands of an untrained person, that same knife could be a dangerous tool. . . . A budget can be effectively used, abused, incorrectly used, or not used at all." The research clarifies the approaches that are successful, and those that are not. This solid guidance is extremely useful, especially because budgeting is so universally practiced—yet so little understood.

There have been few comprehensive studies of budgeting. In fact the last broad study of budget practices was made almost 30 years ago. Clearly the business world has changed a great deal since then. The present research is by far the most comprehensive study ever to be made of budgeting. It is comprehensive in many ways:

Method: The research used real companies and is thorough in approach and application.

Scale: Of the companies studied, more than half exceeded $500 million in sales, but almost 20% were below $50 million.

Range: More than 400 companies were included, from nine industries.

Results: The research findings have value for managers, professors of business, and researchers alike.

Perhaps most important, it is comprehensive in *scope*. This research studies budgeting in combination with the management philosophy, the organization culture, organization development, long-range planning, the corporate and business unit strategies, and strategy implementation. Previous studies of budgeting have focused mainly on the accounting mechanics, or on only a few facets of the complex process of budgeting. But budgets do not exist in a vacuum.

Budgeting involves not only the accounting aspects, but also the people as individuals, people in groups, interaction between groups, and the related organization context. This study is unique in dealing comprehensively with all of these interdependent factors. I believe that is the reason why the past studies have produced only fragmentary and conflicting results and why this study produces comprehensive findings.

In my experience, most large or medium-sized organizations do not differ most significantly in the formal accounting procedures used for budgeting. The big differences appear in the dynamic human and organizational interactions that take place around the budgeting processes. I believe it is these interactions that determine whether the budget becomes merely a ritual, or gravitates into gamesmanship, or attains its potential as a powerful force in organization management. This experience makes the present study ring true for me as a real landmark in the field.

How can any one researcher be qualified to deal with all of the complex and diverse aspects of budgeting in the human, organizational, and accounting context that I have just discussed? Is it not really a project for an interdisciplinary team of experts, working in effective coordination with each other? In my opinion, nothing less could do the job.

Fortunately, the author is just such a team, combined into one person. Professor Umapathy is a remarkable blend of highly expert accountant, plus skilled and experienced organization development consultant. He is a professional member of the NTL Institute and has been a trainer in their widely respected programs. He is prolific and successful as a researcher, and he is a sought-after leader of a wide variety of executive seminars.

As impressive as his credentials are, to me they are still not sufficient to explain the excellence of his budget study. There must be something more. I believe that there is indeed something more. I regard it as creativity and wisdom, mixed with solid practicality. When I consider this book, I think of the following quotations:

> Creativeness often consists of merely turning up what is already there. Did you know that right and left shoes were thought up only a little more than a century ago?
>
> Bernice Fitz-Gibbon

> Research is to see what everybody else has seen, and to think what nobody else has thought.
>
> Albert Szeni-Gyorgyi

Of course it looks easy after it has been done. And the results of this study seem like perfect common sense. But why had no one done it before?

John Leslie Livingstone
Chairman and Professor
Accounting Division
Babson College

Preface

Early in 1974, as a manager in the Corporate Budget Cell of Tata Engineering and Locomotive Co. Ltd., Bombay, India, I used to wonder why budgeting was so unpopular and ineffective, and what could be done to make it more useful to managers. This book is the result of the long process of my "search for the truth." The path I chose was nontraditional because traditional approaches seemed to have led to negligible improvements.

In my search, I conducted an intensive nine-month observation of the budget process in each of two divisions of two large firms. I followed the budget from subdepartmental level to the time it was presented before the board of directors. I learned quickly that the behavioral aspects of budgeting were much more important than the procedural aspects. Since then, I have developed my skills in group dynamics, became a professional member of the NTL Institute (formerly National Training Laboratories), and now use the budgetary process as an entry point for organization development interventions. NTL has a 40-year history of helping people to understand how they can convert their own organizations into high-performance systems.

The Institute has done development work in T-groups, group dynamics, and organizational development.

I believe that budgeting provides managers with a wonderful opportunity to rejuvenate their organizations. There is no other managerial process I am aware of that translates qualitative mission statements and corporate strategies into action plans, links the short-term with the long-term, brings together managers from different hierarchical levels and from different functional areas, and at the same time provides continuity by the sheer regularity of the process.

I have always believed that budgeting can be a powerful tool. The problem is that managers frequently believe that budgets have been imposed on them. Once managers learn that they themselves are the primary beneficiaries of budgeting, their attitudes change instantly. This book recommends some specific approaches to increase budgeting effectiveness. These recommendations can be adopted by any organization.

Although I take full responsibility for any flaws in the book, I would like to acknowledge the contributions made by several persons. The research methodology used in this study is partially based on what I learned from professors Richard F. Vancil and Vijay Sathe, and this study integrates data collected from personal interviews with large sample questionnaire survey data. Vancil and Sathe taught me that I can address both academic and practitioner audiences.

I consider the 1958 book *Business Budgeting* by professors B. H. Sord and G. A. Welsch to be the foundation on which this study was built. I have benefited from reading their book several times.

Professor Robert Chin and Ms. Elsie Y. Cross, members of the NTL Institute, helped me learn about group dynamics and nurtured my skills as an experiential educator. The doctoral seminar of Professor Paul Lawrence has had a profound influence on me, and since I took his seminar, I have always used the contingency and systems perspectives in my research, teaching, and writing. This study has benefited much from the comments and suggestions made by Professor Krishnagopal Menon, my friend and colleague.

Ms. Shelley Schussheim made a significant contribution to this project as research assistant. Her dedication and patience were of enormous help in establishing the computerized data base and analysis. Michael Christian provided superb secretarial services and typed all tables.

Over 400 firms participated in the study, which would not have been possible without the support of the managers who completed the questionnaires.

The National Association of Accountants (NAA) sponsored this study. Mr. Stephen Landekich was the director of research when this research project was initiated, and later Mr. Patrick Romano took over. Both Landekich and Romano were supportive and helped me in every possible way. The Board of Research, Babson College, provided partial financial support when this book was written.

Mr. James R. Dunton, acquisitions editor for Quorum Books, has helped me by responding quickly to my requests and by offering valuable suggestions on how I could help the publisher in minimizing the time taken to convert a manuscript into a book. Todd Adkins and Sandra Wendel made valuable contributions by making the book more easily readable.

I would like to thank my wife, Mala, for the various sacrifices she made throughout the research process and for helping me overcome the ups and downs associated with any large research effort. Our daughter Shalini deserves special thanks for letting me play with the word processor whenever I wanted to.

Finally, I wish to acknowledge that this list is incomplete and that there were many others who made this book possible. Omissions are purely on account of my inability to remember all contributors.

Overview of the Study

INTRODUCTION

This book documents current budgeting practices and suggests how a manager can improve budgetary effectiveness in his or her firm. The book is written for three audiences: managers, accounting researchers, and accounting instructors.

Managers can benefit by understanding current practices and by implementing the specific guidelines (chapter 9) for improving budgetary effectiveness. This study provides accounting researchers with valid data on current practices, and the data base provides many opportunities for further research. The conceptual model of effective planning and control systems (chapter 10) could be a source for developing hypotheses, some of which can be tested using the data generated from the study. Other hypotheses can be tested elsewhere. Chapter 10 shows how to apply the model in the design and use of budgetary controls. The survey data and the model are likely to be useful in the classroom. Simple budgetary tools, like flexible budgeting, are not used widely. Therefore, students should be forewarned that the data they need for using their accounting tools may not be readily available. At the same time, the study demonstrates that there are many challenging opportunities for management accountants in any firm.

I recommend that all readers review the executive summary of the study, which follows below. Managers from the nine industries included in the study (chapter 2) can focus on the budgetary practices in their specific industry. Others may want to identify one or two of the nine industries as being similar to their own. Others may like to use the overall or total column in the tables presenting budgetary practices. Managers interested in only the descriptive part of the study should consider reading chapters 2 through 6. Designers of budgetary controls should focus on chapters 8, 9, and 10. Senior managers who are interested in improving budgetary effectiveness may find chapters 9 and 10 useful.

Accounting researchers will find that chapters 1, 2, 8, 9, and 10 address their questions. Specific parts of chapters 3 through 7 may be helpful to the researchers. The book as a whole will be a useful resource for any management accounting instructor and for students interested in planning and budgetary control systems. This book is likely to be a good reference resource for most students and should be made available in college, university, and public libraries. The questionnaire used in the study (Appendix I) can be modified to create hypothetical case studies of companies with specific budgetary practices. These case studies can serve as the basis for classroom discussion.

EXECUTIVE SUMMARY

Budgeting offers managers a unique opportunity to plan and improve their firms' effectiveness and efficiency. It is probably the only management process that helps integrate the activities of various functional areas, links long-range plans to short-term actions, and simultaneously acts as a vehicle to communicate the views and priorities of top management to other managers.

Managers therefore invest considerable time and energy in developing budgetary goals and in monitoring actuals against the targets. Despite the obvious importance accorded to budgeting, and our extensive experience with budgets, we seem to know very little about budgeting. Practitioner-oriented books and articles on budgeting recommend specific procedure and formalities, but do not present a comprehensive approach to budgeting. Academic literature on budgeting, on the other hand, cannot make specific recommendations since conflicting results are reported in each major aspect of budgeting. Our relative ignorance of budgeting can be traced to two causal factors:

1. Current budgetary practices have not been documented, and we do not know what constitutes effective budgeting.
2. We do not have a comprehensive model of how to prepare and use budgets effectively.

Based on the responses from 402 firms representing nine industries, this study is aimed at improving our knowledge in these two areas.

Chapter 1: Research Objectives and Methodology

The primary objective of this study is to describe current budgetary practices in large- and medium-sized firms in the United States. Concomitant with this objective, this study has been designed to do the following:

1. Document current budget practices and procedures in the United States.
2. Examine whether there are significant variations in budget practices across different industries.
3. Describe the qualifications and experiences of budget managers in different industries.
4. Compare and contrast the results of this study with those of the study of Sord and Welsch published in 1958.
5. Determine the nature and extent of variations in budgetary practices with selected dimensions of company characteristics and management philosophy.
6. Analyze whether budgetary practices of financially successful firms are different from those of other companies.

7. Discuss the implications of current budgetary practices for practitioners and researchers.

In order to build a strong foundation in the form of valid data on current budgetary practices, it is necessary to include a large number of firms from several industries. Mail survey was therefore selected as the most appropriate method of data collection. Based on a pretest sample of 30 firms, of whom 17 responded, the questionnaire was finalized (Appendix I). The questionnaire is divided into five parts: company characteristics, management philosophy, long-range planning, budgeting, and budget manager. Secondary data were collected on selected company characteristics including geographical location, sales, assets, number of employees, return on equity, major product line, extent of diversification, and price-to-earnings ratio.

Chapter 2: Characteristics of the Participants

The questionnaire was mailed to a sample of 1,006 large and medium firms from nine different industries. This study is based on the 402 usable responses received (a response rate of 40%). This response rate is comparable to or better than similar national surveys. The distribution of sample size and responses by industry is as follows:

Industry	Sample Size	Responses
Commercial Banks	100	50
Diversified Finance Companies	48	15
Diversified Service Companies	49	22
Hospitals in Massachusetts	100	36
Life Insurance Companies	50	26
Large-Size Manufacturing Firms	242	108
Medium-Size Manufacturing Firms	135	42
Retail/Wholesale Trade	97	29
Transportation	50	17
Utilities	50	28
Miscellaneous	85	29
	1006	402

Some key demographic characteristics of the sample are as follows. The survey respondents are primarily from larger firms, with about 55% of the respondents having over $500 million of sales, and 19% with a sales level of less than $50 million. Half of the participants have fewer than 5,000 employees, while 17% have over 25,000 employees each. Nearly half the participants are engaged in products or services represented by one two-digit Standard Industrial Classification Code, with companies in the manufacturing and diversified service industries reporting high levels of diversity.

Nearly 40% of the firms have overseas operations, more so in the diversified service and large manufacturing sectors. Over 90% of the participants classify themselves as growing, while only 1% of the companies describe themselves as shrinking. Commercial banks, diversified finance, and life insurance companies rate themselves as facing a high rate of change. Utilities, retail, and diversified service industries state that they operate in a relatively stable environment. Intracompany transfers took place in about 70% of the firms. These transfers were relatively more popular in the manufacturing and retail industries. Only 7% of the respondents state that they are losing money, and slightly over 50% of the firms rate themselves as being more profitable than comparable companies.

Nearly all (97%) the participants have a formal budget program. Over 90% of the firms in commercial banking, diversified service, large manufacturing, and retail industries use profit centers. However, only 27% of hospitals use profit centers. Most of the firms with a formal budget program used a 12-month budget period. A partial list of the participants is presented in Appendix II.

Chapter 3: Management Philosophy and Budgeting

The top management of each company has unique beliefs about how the company should be managed. These beliefs are directly reflected in both the design and use of budgets, and budget meetings are frequently used by the top management to communicate and reinforce these beliefs. Major views and assumptions of the top management are summarized here:

1. Multiple approvals for budgets are desirable.
2. A bottom-up goal-setting process should be used.

3. Both financial and nonfinancial targets should be used.

4. Financial targets should be difficult in order to be effective.

5. Budgets used for planning and coordination can also be used for evaluation purposes.

6. It is appropriate to review budgets for possible revision of goals for planning and coordination; however, budgets used for evaluating managers should not be revised.

7. Both quantitative and qualitative data should be used to evaluate managers; however, more importance should be given to quantitative data.

8. Computers should be used extensively, especially for preparing budgets and performance reports. Profit centers' computers should be compatible with corporate computers. Profit center managers should have direct access to their data bases.

9. Budgets should serve several purposes. The relative importance of the uses in decreasing order are coordinating various activities, planning, evaluating, communicating priorities of the top management, motivating managers, compensating managers, and educating and developing managers.

10. Budgets should be used to motivate subordinates to increase output and efficiency by encouraging their participation during budget preparation. Budgets should not be used to exert pressure on subordinates.

11. Formal meetings between corporate and lower-level managers are important. Monthly meetings are preferable.

12. It is important to subdivide a firm into profit centers and to vary budget policies and procedures across profit centers.

13. Budget is the most important organizational device to manage corporate-divisional relationships. Other major devices are capital budgets, informal contacts between corporate and profit center managers, and performance evaluation systems. It is desirable to use several organizational devices.

These top management views confirm the perceived importance of budgets. It is also clear that top management is interested in generating commitment to budgetary targets by including nonfinancial targets and by making budgeting a bottom-up process. The data suggest that these commitment-building activities may be thwarted by the top management obsession with the use of difficult quantitative targets.

Chapter 4: Long-Range Planning Practices

About three-fourths of the participants use comprehensive long-range planning systems. Most firms develop long-range goals in several areas and update them annually. Long-range plans are prepared at the profit center level in three-fourths of the firms.

Despite the importance given to long-range plans, there seems to be an unintended bias in favor of short-term planning. The short-term bias is reflected in the time horizon chosen for long-term planning, in the preferred practice of establishing tight linkages between long- and short-term plans, and in the annual review of long-term plan targets. It is therefore likely that in many companies long-term plans are mere extrapolations of the annual budget.

Most utility, manufacturing, diversified service, and transportation firms adopt a plan period of four years or more. Commercial banks and hospitals do not give adequate emphasis to long-range planning. Industries lagging behind in long-range planning can benefit by selective adoption of the techniques used by the leading industries and by offering training programs to their managers to develop skills in developing long-range plans and in linking them to budgets.

Chapter 5: Budgetary Practices in the United States

The data on budgetary practices in each industry are grouped into the following six broad categories:

Forecasting

Budgetary policies and procedures

Budgetary standards

Performance reports

Consequences of budgeting

Self-perceptions of budgetary effectiveness

Forecasting

Preparation of a forecast is the starting point in the budgetary process. The use of a forecast acceptable to the responsible manager is a prerequisite for effective budgeting. The survey data suggest that most firms prepare forecasts of company sales only. Forecasts of general economic conditions, industry sales, and market share are used less frequently. Diversified financial and manufacturing firms frequently use more than one method of forecasting and have established sophisticated forecasting systems.

Analysis of historical data and opinions of company managers are used by three-fourths of the participants for long-range planning and by almost everyone for preparing sales forecasts used in budgeting. Economic models are used by about 60% of the participants for both long-range planning and budgeting. Industry analysis is used by 85% of the respondents for budgeting and by over 50% for long-range planning. Consultants are rarely used in preparing forecasts for either long-range plans or budgets.

In general, the respondents stress internal sources of information for preparing long- and short-term sales forecasts. Managers in dynamic industries should examine whether increased emphasis on external sources of information will improve the accuracy of sales forecasts.

Budgetary Policies and Procedures

Budgeting is rated as the most important organizational device for managing corporate and profit center relationships. Given that most firms prepare budgets over a four-month period, budgeting is a major project. However, managers rarely use proven techniques of project management, such as Critical Path Method (CPM) or Program Evaluation and Review Technique (PERT), to schedule and monitor the preparation of budgets.

Budget manuals are used by nearly two-thirds of the firms, and about 90% of the respondents use preprinted budget forms. In contrast, only 40% of the participants use a formal procedure to evaluate the effectiveness of preparing and using budgets. Two-thirds of the participants use detailed and comprehensive procedures for over 60% of the budgeting activities.

Although several budgeting techniques were originally developed in the manufacturing sector, the data suggest that manufacturing firms are no longer at the leading edge of budgeting technology. Diversified financial firms, for example, have adopted sophisticated formal budgetary processes more readily than other industries.

Nearly 60% of the firms state that they made significant changes in their budgetary processes during the past three years. Given the long history of budgeting, it is surprising that such a high proportion of companies report that they made significant changes in their budgetary controls. The recessionary trends in the U.S. economy from 1981 to 1984, as well as the perceived need for improving profitability through budgeting, have contributed to the observed changes in budgetary practices.

Budgetary Standards

Approximately 70% of the participants use two or three sources to specify revenue standards, of which the sales budget is the most popular source. Use of historical costs (80%) and budgets for overhead expenses (73%) were the major sources for establishing standards for costs and expenses. Over 50% of the respondents use six or more sources for setting standards for costs and expenses. Companies seem to place a heavy emphasis on standard setting and apparently believe that the use of multiple sources of information for establishing standards is desirable. Some managers may be using too much information during the standard setting process.

Top management emphasizes formal processes in communicating responsibilities to senior managers, while informal conferences provide the major communication channel between middle- and lower-level managers. Budgets are usually prepared annually and are broken down by quarters. Although most managerial accounting texts strongly advocate the use of flexible budgets, only 27% of the respondents use flexible budgeting. Expenses are classified into controllable and noncontrollable categories in 54% of the firms. Contingency plans and rolling budgets are used in 34% and 21% of the firms respectively. Budgets are subdivided by product lines in about 60% of the firms.

Despite significant changes introduced by 60% of the firms during the past three years, it is surprising that these simple techniques of budgeting are not used in many firms. Budgets are, however, subdivided by major organizational subunits in over 90% of the firms. The analysis suggests there is ample room for improving the level of sophistication of budgetary procedures in the industry, especially in the service sector.

Performance Reports

Over 90% of the firms prepare a separate performance report for each department or profit center. However, nearly 30% of the participants report that in their firms there is an insufficient match between the responsibility structure and the performance reports. Budgetary targets are frequently broken down by quarters, while performance reports are usually prepared each month. Improved matching of the responsibility structure and time periods used in setting targets and in performance reporting should be encouraged. Written explanation of the causes of significant variances (67%) and discussion of the deviations with the immediate superior (56%) are the most popular approaches used in reacting to variances.

Consequences of Budgeting

This study reveals that budget games are widely practiced. Deferring a needed expenditure is the most popular budget game. Getting approvals after money was spent, shifting funds between accounts to avoid budget overruns, and employing contract labor to avoid exceeding headcount limits are the other relatively popular games. Nearly all respondents engage in one or more budget games. Managers in these firms either did not accept the budgetary targets and opted to beat the system, or they felt pressured to achieve the targets at any cost. The wide prevalence of budget games suggests that budgetary processes in the industry are suboptimal and that managers are not committed to budgetary goals.

Self-Perceptions of Budgetary Effectiveness

Nearly 80% of the respondents rate their budgetary effectiveness as either good or extremely effective. Although the data on current budgetary practices suggest that some simple techniques of budgeting can be introduced and that managers are being given difficult and unacceptable targets, budget managers consider their budgeting to be effective. Perhaps they believe that no major improvements can be made and have become complacent with the quality of budgeting in their companies.

Chapter 6: Budget Manager Characteristics

The titles given to budget managers and their reporting relationships suggest that they occupy a reasonable high corporate position in most firms. Only 18% of the participating firms established the budget manager's position after 1981. Budgeting is in its infancy in transportation and diversified finance companies, and budget managers were appointed in these two industries quite recently. Budget managers seem to have substantial training in accounting or finance, but nearly 40% of the budget managers have no nonfinancial experience. This bias may be unfortunate, since good budget managers should understand the characteristics of their businesses and should possess excellent interpersonal, communication, and negotiation skills.

It is unlikely that the traditional accounting or business curricula emphasize these skill areas. Hence, the possibility of recruiting budget managers from nonfinancial areas of specialization should be explored. It is also desirable to develop special training modules so that these managers can refine their skills in selected areas.

Coordinating the preparation of the budget and monitoring performance against the budget consumes a high proportion of a budget manager's time. Apparently, the budget manager's role is being perceived as advisory, and corrective actions are taken by line managers. The scope for increasing a budget manager's role in follow-up and corrective action should be explored. Each firm needs to examine whether it has defined the budget manager's role appropriately.

Chapter 7: Changes in Budgetary Practices during the Period 1958-1984

Sord and Welsch published the results of a comprehensive study of budgetary practices in 1958. It is gratifying to note that budgeting is currently used by almost all firms, that more frequent reviews of budgets are undertaken, and that more target areas are specified by a larger proportion of firms in their long-term plans. In contrast, the following changes may be undesirable:

1. Decreased emphasis on the use of committees and informal processes to discuss variances with immediate superiors
2. Increased frequency of reviews for possible revision of goals, which could lead to decreased commitment to specific goals
3. Increasing trend toward a top-down process and toward imposing more pressure on managers during the budgetary process
4. Tendency to use more sources of information and more analytical tools to prepare forecasts, possibly leading to conflicting conclusions
5. Increased reliance on internally generated data in developing standards for both revenues and expenses
6. Increase in the proportion of firms having a misfit between the responsibility structure and performance reporting systems
7. Decreased use of simple, yet proven, techniques of management accounting, such as the use of flexible budgets, classifying costs into controllable and noncontrollable categories, and subdividing the budget by product lines
8. Increased reliance on using persons with specialized experience in accounting or finance for appointment as budget managers, and treating a budget manager's job as a stepping-stone and not as a career

Although these trends can be reversed easily, budgeting is so repetitive and so procedurally oriented that the managers may be unaware of the presence of these undesirable trends. Each company should conduct a comprehensive audit of its budgets from time to time, so that healthy budgetary practices can be fostered, and undesirable practices can be weeded out.

Chapter 8: Company Characteristics and Budgetary Practices

An analysis of the relationships between company characteristics and budgetary processes revealed some statistically significant correlations. The following five situational factors, which were statistically relevant, seem to be related to a comprehensive measure of the degree of complexity of the firm:

Size: Larger organizations are more complex.

Diversification: Firms that are more diversified are more complex.

Company Strategy: Growth-oriented firms are more complex.

Rate of Change: Rapidly changing firms are more complex.

Level of Interdependence: Firms with highly interdependent units are more complex.

Designers of budgetary control systems should first assess the degree of complexity of an organization, using the five factors just listed. Complex organizations require sophisticated budgetary controls. Managers should attempt to improve the effectiveness of their budgetary controls by selectively adopting budgetary practices used by effective firms of comparable complexity. Companies with a higher degree of complexity should adopt the following practices:

1. Use budgets for a variety of purposes, such as planning, coordinating, motivating, evaluating, communicating, compensating, and educating managers.

2. Build strong linkages between the long-term plans and the short-term budgets.

3. Review budgets for possible revision of goals, either for planning or for evaluation purposes.

4. Use detailed and comprehensive procedures for a high proportion of budgeting activities and match control reports with each manager's authority and responsibility.

5. Use techniques such as Gantt charts or Critical Path Method for scheduling and monitoring the preparation of budgets.

6. Use techniques such as flexible budgeting, classification of expenses into controllable and noncontrollable categories, preparation of contingency plans and rolling budgets, and subdividing budget by product lines and by major subunits of the firm.

7. Use reports comparing actual performance with standards of performance or budget objectives prepared for each profit center.

8. Anticipate the likelihood of more budget games and take steps to minimize such dysfunctional behavior.

Chapter 9: Budgetary Practices in Successful Firms

Financially successful firms used budgetary practices that were different from other firms. The analyses suggest that any firm interested in improving its performance should adopt the following practices:

1. Use several nonfinancial targets.
2. Use reasonable budgetary targets.
3. Review budgets for possible revision of goals for evaluation purposes.
4. Use budgets for planning, coordinating, motivating, evaluating, determining managerial compensation, communicating top management's priorities, and educating managers.
5. Establish linkages between the long- and short-term plans.
6. Use scheduling techniques to monitor budget preparation.
7. Use formal procedures to evaluate budgetary effectiveness.
8. Use detailed and comprehensive procedures for a large proportion of budgetary activities.
9. Create a fit between performance reports and the responsibilities of each manager.
10. Increase the degree of sophistication of the budgetary process by introducing budgeting techniques such as flexible budgeting, contingency planning, preparation of rolling budgets, subdividing budgets by organizational subunits.
11. Ask managers to furnish written explanations for deviations from budgets, as well as indicate corrective actions taken.
12. Discourage managers from engaging in budget games.
13. Employ a qualified budget manager and assign a senior title to the manager.
14. Spend more time in follow-up and corrective action.

By adopting these practices, any firm can improve its performance.

Chapter 10: Implications for Managers and Academics

A conceptual model of effective planning and control systems is presented in chapter 10. The basic premise of the model is that long-term plans should be prepared before undertaking short-term planning. Thus, defining the mission facilitates the development of goals, and a clear set of goals is needed for establishing meaningful objectives. Once the objectives are finalized, strategies, programs, and budgets can be prepared in a chronological sequence. The findings of this study support the predictions of the model. The chapter also provides guidelines on how to use the model to improve budgetary effectiveness in any firm.

A major conclusion of the study is that budgeting is a self-fulfilling prophecy. Companies that believe that budgeting is a powerful tool take the trouble to design the controls to match organizational needs, to use the controls effectively, and to achieve high levels of performance. In contrast, firms that do not believe in budgets pay lip service to design and use of budgetary controls, literally invite their managers to play budget games, and finally blame the budgets for the poor results. Thus, organizations seem to inherit the budgetary processes they want.

CURRENT BUDGETING
PRACTICES IN
U.S. INDUSTRY

1

Research Objectives and Methodology

Budgeting is probably the most powerful managerial process. It is the only activity that regularly brings together managers from different functional areas and hierarchical levels. Budgeting helps in translating long- and medium-term plans into specific short-term activities, as well as in assigning responsibilities for the activities to specific managers. The questions raised and the issues discussed in budget meetings serve to communicate the values, beliefs, and priorities of the top management to other managers. The budgetary process is rhythmic and encompasses the entire organization. It is therefore a natural entry point for introducing changes in a firm. These characteristics of budgeting have contributed to its popularity.

Several studies have confirmed that most U.S. firms use budgetary controls and that they compared actual results with budgets on a regular basis. Although budgeting has been used regularly in most firms for several years and managers invest considerable time and energy in preparing and using budgets, as Hopwood points out, we know very little about budgeting.

Despite its wide acceptance, budgeting remains one of the most intriguing and perplexing of management accounting procedures. With many fundamental questions remaining unsolved, it provides an ideal focus for considering some of the social and human factors which influence the operation of accounting systems in complex organizations.[1]

Several scholars have noted the importance of budgeting and have conducted much related research. However, the results to date have been difficult to integrate and often conflicting. Academic research in budgeting has therefore not been able to provide reliable answers to practitioners' queries on how one should prepare and use budgets. The most recent comprehensive description of budget practices in U.S. firms is the 1958 study by Sord and Welsch.[2]

We know very little about the changes that have taken place in budgetary practices in the way firms operate. These changes in the business environment include the following:

1. Increase in size, product diversity, and geographical dispersion in firms
2. Increased use of computers, especially during the past five years after the introduction of microcomputers
3. Increased use of decentralization as a common form of organization
4. Improved systems of communication
5. A substantial increase in professionally qualified managers
6. Improvements in formal planning and control systems, especially strategic planning

Obviously, these changes would have had a direct impact on budget practices. However, we are aware of neither the current practices in budgeting, nor the major changes in budget practices since 1958. Despite the widely acknowledged importance of budgeting, we do not have a comprehensive model of how to prepare and use budgets. This study increases our knowledge in this important area.

PURPOSE OF THE STUDY

This study describes current budgetary practices in large- and medium-sized firms in the United States. Concomitant with this objective, this study has been designed to do the following:

1. Document current budget practices and procedures in U.S. firms.
2. Examine whether there are significant variations in budget practices across different industries.
3. Describe the qualifications and experience of the budget manager in different industries.
4. Compare and contrast the results of this study with those of the study by Sord and Welsch.
5. Determine the nature and extent of variations in budgetary practices with selected dimensions of company characteristics and management philosophy.
6. Analyze whether the budgetary practices of financially successful firms are different from those of other companies.
7. Discuss the implications of this study for practitioners and researchers.

SIGNIFICANCE OF THE STUDY

Given that most firms have used budgeting for several years, and that each year managers invest considerable time and energy in the preparation and use of budgets, one would expect budgeting to be a highly standardized and highly mechanized activity. The plethora of books and articles on budgeting also suggests that we know the "right" way to prepare and use budgets, and that although budgeting is important, it may be a relatively easy and routine activity.

Nothing can be further from the truth. Neither the practitioners nor the academics are aware of current budgetary practices, and hard data on budget practices have been confined to reports on selected aspects of budgeting in a specific company, or in a few companies. This book reports on the most comprehensive study of budgeting, both in terms of the sample size and the topics included. The results of this study should be of interest to both designers and users of budgetary control systems, and managers can use the information in assessing the extent of sophistication of the budgetary practices in their respective firms. Academics can use the results in teaching students current practices in budgeting and in identifying topics or hypotheses for future research.

LITERATURE REVIEW

A literature review was undertaken to assess the current knowledge base in budgeting. The literature on budgeting could be classified into three broad categories: accounting view of budgeting; behavioral studies in budgeting; and surveys of budgetary practices.

Accounting View of Budgeting

Most textbooks in managerial accounting, and many practitioner-oriented books and articles describing how to set up and operate a budgetary control system, have contributed to the accounting view of budgeting. These books and articles make the basic concepts behind budgeting simple enough for easy understanding, and they focus on the procedures to be followed. Although some of these publications expose their readers to selected sophisticated budgeting techniques, the extent to which such techniques are used in the industry remains unknown.

Johnson observed that the bulk of the literature dealing with budgets and budgeting "talks in words which may be associated with accounting, decision theory and economics."[3] Hofstede noted that the accounting theory of budgeting is a direct descendant of the traditional organization theory: It believes in one best way of behavior that could be thought out by specialists, learned by individuals, and maintained by appropriate material incentives. Hofstede concluded that the accounting view of budgeting made simplistic assumptions about human behavior and suggested that one should start viewing organizations empirically rather than using a normative approach.[4]

Behavioral Studies in Budgeting

Behavioral studies recognize that budgeting techniques and procedures are only a means to an end. The primary objective of budgeting and other planning and control systems is to help managers in allocating organizational resources effectively and efficiently. Several studies have concluded that resource allocation and similar complex organizational decisions are not made on a purely rational basis.[5]

Given the complexity of budgetary processes in most medium to large firms, researchers have attempted to simplify the problem by focusing either on the micro level (such as the level of an individual manager or on macro-level attributes (such as type of organization). A major portion of the literature on the behavioral aspects of accounting is at a micro level of analysis and focuses on individuals. Major areas of such research include motivation, participation, goal difficulty, manager's personality, leadership style, decision making, and dysfunctional consequences of budgeting. Merchant concluded that it is difficult to integrate these micro-level studies, since their results are often conflicting.

Further, there has been little accounting-related research conducted above the individual level of analysis. Integrating micro-and macro-level studies in budgeting is therefore a formidable task. Although budget-related activities are usually carried out in small groups, and interpersonal relationships play a crucial role in establishing budgetary targets, behavioral research on interpersonal and small group behavior has not been incorporated in the accounting literature on budgeting.

Surveys of Budgetary Practices

Sord and Welsch conducted a survey of budgetary controls in different industries. Their study covered 389 companies through a mail survey and 35 companies through personal interviews. Although several recent surveys examine either one aspect of budgetary control, such as performance evaluation or budgetary practices in a few selected firms, the Sord and Welsch survey published in 1958 is the most recent study of budgetary practices.

In summary, although it is widely recognized that budgeting is important, we do not know how firms in different industries prepare and use budgets. Neither are we aware of the characteristics of effective budgeting. The methodology chosen for this study recognizes the limited pool of knowledge on budgeting available to practitioners and academics.

RESEARCH METHODOLOGY

The methodology used in this study aims at building a strong foundation in the form of valid data on current budgeting practices to serve the needs of both practitioners and academics. In order to include a large number of firms from several industries, the use of mail questionnaires was selected as the most appropriate method of data collection.

A mail questionnaire was developed and mailed to a pretest sample of 30 firms in Boston and New York. The pretest sample included manufacturing, wholesale/retail trade, finance, insurance, and banking industries. The questionnaire was sent along with a cover letter from the Director of Research of the NAA, and a reminder was sent after two weeks. Eleven responses were received within two weeks, and six more companies responded after receiving a reminder. One of the addresses had moved, so that the response rate in the pretest survey was 59% (17 out of 29). All the industries were well represented in the returned questionnaires.

Most medium-sized companies did not respond. The responses received from the medium-sized sector indicated that some of them did not have a long-range planning system and that their budgetary controls were not as sophisticated as those in the larger companies. The medium-sized firms were probably emphasizing informal uses of budgets. The poor response rate from the medium-sized firms may be explained by the fact that a questionnaire cannot be used to collect sufficient data on informal processes and that the managers receiving the questionnaire were not motivated to complete it. This suggested that only firms that emphasize formal aspects of budgeting were likely to participate in the study.

The high response rate from both manufacturing and non-manufacturing sectors suggested that the questionnaire was suitable for use in both types of organizations.

Based on pretest results, the researcher decided to increase the representation of larger firms. The emphasis on medium-sized firms was decreased because of the expected lower response rate and difficulty in making comparisons across firms because of wide differences in management styles, strategies, and product mix. The study was expanded to include additional nonmanufacturing sectors: transportation, utilities, hospitals, diversified finance, and diversified services. Also, some questions were modified in order to make the questionnaire easier to understand. Questions that did not seem to add much value were dropped. The final questionnaire used in the survey is presented along with a summary of responses in Appendix I.

The sample for the mail questionnaires and response rate is presented in Table 1. The larger companies in the sample were selected from the Fortune 500 and the Fortune Service 500 lists. Medium-sized firms were selected from the Standard and Poor's Directory in specific Standard Industry Classification (SIC) categories. A state-by-state listing of hospitals published by the American Hospital Association was used in selecting a sample of 100 hospitals in Massachusetts and 50 hospitals in California.

A comparison of some overall parameters describing the scope and coverage of this study and the 1958 study by Sord and Welsch is presented in Table 2.

The questionnaire was broadly divided into five parts:

Part I   Company Characteristics

Part II   Management Philosophy

Part III   Long-Range Planning

Part IV   Budgeting

Part V   Budget Manager

Secondary data were collected on geographical location, sales, assets, number of employees, return on equity, SIC code for the

Table 1
Response to the Mail Survey on Budget Practices

	Industry	Sample Size	Responses No.	Responses %	Percentage Response
1.	Commercial Banks	100	50	12.4	50.0%
2.	Diversified Finance Companies	48	15	3.7	31.3%
3.	Diversified Service Companies	49	22	5.5	44.9%
4.	Hospitals in Massachusetts	100	36	9.0	36.0%
5.	Life Insurance Companies	50	26	6.5	52.0%
6.	Large-Size Manufacturing Firms	242	108	26.9	44.6%
7.	Medium-Size Manufacturing Firms	135	42	10.4	31.1%
8.	Retail/Wholesale Trade	97	29	7.2	29.9%
9.	Transportation	50	17	4.2	34.0%
10.	Utilities	50	28	7.0	56.0%
	Sub Total	921	373	92.8	40.5%
11.	Miscellaneous	85	29*	7.2	34.1%
	Grand Total	1006	402**	100.0	40.0%

* Includes 5 hospitals from California.
** Excludes 9 incomplete responses.

Table 2
A Comparison of Some Broad Parameters of this Survey with Those of the Sord and Welsch Study (1958)

	Parameter	This Study	Sord and Welsch Study
1.	Number of Questionnaires Mailed	1006	765
2.	Completed Questionnaires Included in the Study	402	389
3.	Number of Industry Classifications Used	11	6
4.	Number of Pages in the Questionnaire	7	4
5.	Pretest Sample	29	20
6.	Number of Responses to the Pretest Questionnaire	17	15
7.	Total Number of Firms Participating in the Study	419	404

major product line, extent of diversification, and price-to-earnings ratio for each of the respondents. The results of the questionnaire survey are presented industrywide, so that variations in budget practices across different industries could be readily seen.

THE STRUCTURE OF THE BOOK

Each of the following five chapters in turn focuses on the five parts of the questionnaire. The seventh chapter compares the state of the art of budgeting in 1958 (Sord and Welsch) with current budgetary practices. The eighth chapter describes the observed relationships between company characteristics and budgetary practices and develops an approach to design budgetary controls based on company characteristics. The ninth chapter identifies budgetary practices that are correlated with measures of performance. Based on the analysis, specific recommendations are made to fine tune budgetary practices and improve performance. Finally, the tenth chapter presents a conceptual model of effective budgetary practices and discusses the implications of this study for practitioners and academics.

NOTES

1. A. F. Hopwood, *Accounting and Human Behavior* (London: Haymarket Publishing Limited, 1974), p. 39.

2. B. H. Sord and G. A. Welsch, *Business Budgeting* (New York: Controllership Foundation, Inc., 1958).

3. G. G. Johnson, *The Role of Formal Evaluation in the Process of Budgetary Control,* Unpublished dissertation, Harvard Business School, 1972.

4. G. H. Hofstede, *The Game of Budget Control* (Assen, Neth.: Van Gorcum, 1967).

5. C. P. Bonini, *Simulation of Information and Decision Systems in the Firm* (Englewood Cliffs, NJ: Prentice Hall, Inc., 1963); W. J. Bruns, "Accounting Information and Decision Making: Some Behavioral Hypotheses," *The Accounting Review* (July 1968), pp. 469-480; C. W. Churchman, *Prediction and Optimal Decision* (Englewood Cliffs, NJ: Prentice Hall, Inc., 1961).

6. K. A. Merchant, "The Design of the Corporate Budgeting System: Influences on Managerial Behavior and Performance," *The Accounting Review* (October 1981), pp. 813-829.

2

Characteristics of the Participants

This chapter describes some characteristics of the 402 companies included in the study. This information is from Part I of the questionnaire (Questions 1 to 5), as well as from some secondary data on the respondents such as size, major product line, extent of diversification, and profitability. A list of companies that authorized us to identify them as participants is presented in Appendix II. The industries included in this study are commercial banks, diversified finance, diversified service, hospitals, life insurance, manufacturing: large firms, manufacturing: medium-size companies, retail/wholesale trade, transportation, and utilities.

Some firms in the sample which could not be classified into any of these industries, along with completed responses which did not identify the respondent, were included in the miscellaneous group. It is difficult to interpret the data for this group. Selected demographic characteristics of the participating firms are presented by industry the remaining part of this chapter.

SIZE OF THE PARTICIPATING FIRMS

Variations among the participating firms on the sales dimension are presented by industry in Table 3. The numbers used for commercial banks and insurance companies represent interest and other income, and insurance premium and interest income, respectively. Although the survey respondents are primarily from larger firms, with about 55% of the respondents having over $500 million in sales, nearly 19% of the firms are relatively small, with less than $50 million in sales.

Approximately half of the firms have fewer than 5,000 employees (Table 4). A significant majority of the firms in commercial banking, diversified finance, life insurance, and medium-sized manufacturing industries belong to this group. Diversified service, large manufacturing, retail/wholesale trade, and transportation industries comprise the larger employers with over 25,000 employees. About 17% of the respondents have over 25,000 employees each.

EXTENT OF DIVERSIFICATION

The number of two-digit Standard Industrial Classification (SIC) codes for the products or services offered by a company was used to measure the extent of diversification. The greater the number of two-digit SIC codes, the greater the extent of diversification. Nearly half the participants are engaged in products or services represented by one two-digit SIC code. Companies in the manufacturing and diversified service industries are the most diversified in the sample. In general, larger business firms were more diversified than the smaller firms.

PRESENCE OF OVERSEAS OPERATIONS

Nearly 40% of the respondents have overseas operations. A majority of diversified service and large manufacturing firms have foreign operations, while hospitals, life insurance, retail, and utilities sectors typically refrained from operating abroad.

Table 3
Profile of Participating Firms by Industry and Sales Level

Sales Level in $ Millions	Commercial Banks	Diversified Financial	Diversified Service	Hospitals	Life Insurance	Large Manufacturing	Medium Manufacturing	Retailers/Wholesalers	Transportation	Utilities	Miscellaneous	Total
Less than 10	12 (24)	0 (0)	1 (5)	9 (22)	0 (0)	2 (2)	5 (12)	1 (3)	2 (12)	0 (0)	23 (96)	55 (14)
10 – 24	0 (0)	0 (0)	0 (0)	7 (17)	0 (0)	0 (0)	0 (0)	0 (0)	0 (0)	0 (0)	0 (0)	7 (2)
25 – 49	0 (0)	0 (0)	0 (0)	11 (27)	0 (0)	0 (0)	2 (5)	0 (0)	0 (0)	0 (0)	0 (0)	13 (3)
50 – 99	1 (2)	0 (0)	0 (0)	10 (25)	3 (12)	0 (0)	12 (29)	3 (11)	0 (0)	0 (0)	0 (0)	26 (6)
100 – 249	7 (14)	2 (13)	0 (0)	2 (5)	3 (11)	0 (0)	12 (28)	4 (14)	0 (0)	0 (0)	0 (0)	30 (8)
250 – 499	9 (18)	3 (20)	0 (0)	1 (2)	3 (11)	13 (12)	10 (24)	5 (17)	3 (18)	0 (0)	0 (0)	47 (12)
500 – 999	5 (10)	4 (27)	9 (41)	0 (0)	9 (35)	24 (22)	1 (2)	2 (7)	4 (23)	0 (0)	0 (0)	58 (14)
1000 and over	16 (32)	6 (40)	12 (54)	1 (2)	11 (42)	69 (64)	0 (0)	14 (48)	8 (47)	28 (100)	1 (4)	166 (41)
Total	50 (100)	15 (100)	22 (100)	41 (100)	26 (100)	108 (100)	42 (100)	29 (100)	17 (100)	28 (100)	24 (100)	402 (100)

The entries in each cell are "number of respondents" and ("column percentage") respectively.

Table 4
Profile of Participating Firms by Industry and Number of Employees

Number of Employees ('00s)	Commercial Banks	Diversified Financial	Diversified Service	Hospitals	Life Insurance	Large Manufacturing	Medium Manufacturing	Retailers/ Wholesalers	Transportation	Utilities	Miscellaneous	Total
Less than 10	8 (16)	2 (13)	2 (9)	24 (58)	4 (15)	3 (3)	13 (31)	3 (10)	4 (24)	0 (0)	23 (96)	86 (21)
10 – 24	16 (32)	4 (27)	2 (9)	14 (34)	10 (38)	2 (2)	12 (28)	4 (14)	1 (6)	0 (0)	0 (0)	65 (16)
25 – 49	14 (28)	2 (13)	5 (23)	1 (3)	4 (16)	12 (11)	10 (24)	4 (14)	4 (23)	2 (7)	0 (0)	58 (15)
50 – 99	7 (14)	3 (20)	0 (0)	1 (2)	2 (8)	20 (18)	7 (17)	4 (14)	0 (0)	9 (32)	0 (0)	53 (13)
100 – 249	3 (6)	3 (20)	6 (27)	1 (3)	4 (15)	37 (34)	0 (0)	2 (7)	3 (18)	14 (50)	0 (0)	73 (18)
250 – 499	1 (2)	1 (7)	5 (23)	0 (0)	1 (4)	17 (16)	0 (0)	7 (24)	4 (23)	1 (4)	0 (0)	37 (9)
500 – 999	1 (2)	0 (0)	1 (5)	0 (0)	1 (4)	14 (13)	0 (0)	3 (10)	1 (6)	0 (0)	1 (4)	22 (6)
1000 & over	0 (0)	0 (0)	1 (4)	0 (0)	0 (0)	3 (3)	0 (0)	2 (7)	0 (0)	2 (7)	0 (0)	8 (2)
Total	50 (100)	15 (100)	22 (100)	41 (100)	26 (100)	108 (100)	42 (100)	29 (100)	17 (100)	28 (100)	24 (100)	402 (100)

The entries in each cell are "number of respondents" and ("column percentage") respectively.

STRATEGIC MISSION

The first question in Part I of the questionnaire asked the respondents to specify their strategic mission by stating whether they were growing, maintaining at a stable level, or shrinking their operations. Growth-oriented firms were also asked whether they were growing primarily through acquisitions or from within. Over 90% of the participants classify themselves as growing. Growth from within, either at a high rate or on a selective basis, is the strategic mission of 70% of the respondents (Table 5). Selective growth from within seems to be the popular choice across all industries. Only 1% of the companies describe themselves as shrinking their operations.

RATE OF CHANGE IN THE BUSINESS ENVIRONMENT

A composite index of the rate of change in the business environment was computed using the 10 dimensions identified in Question 2. The 10 dimensions of the rate of change in the business environment are product/service characteristics, market demand, distribution network, competitors' strategies, technical developments, production processes, government's economic policies and regulations, labor unions' actions, human resources, and availability of raw materials and other resources. The responses to the dimension "industry pricing patterns" were insufficient and were therefore excluded from the analyses. The composite index of the rate of change for a company was the sum of ratings for each of the dimensions. The minimum and maximum scores for the composite index are 10 and 50, respectively. Larger scores are associated with more change. Commercial banks, diversified finance, and life insurance companies rated themselves as facing a high rate of change (Table 6). Utilities, retail, and diversified service industries rate themselves as operating in a relatively stable environment.

LEVEL OF INTERDEPENDENCE

The level of intracompany sales as a percentage of total company sales was used as a surrogate or level of interdependence within a company (Question 3). There are no intra-

Table 5
Strategic Mission of Respondents by Industry (Question 1)

Strategic Mission	Commercial Banks	Diversified Financial	Diversified Service	Hospitals	Life Insurance	Large Manufacturing	Medium Manufacturing	Retailers/ Wholesalers	Transportation	Utilities	Miscellaneous	Total
Growth through acquisitions	7 (14)	2 (13)	1 (5)	0 (0)	1 (4)	3 (3)	1 (3)	0 (0)	1 (6)	0 (0)	0 (0)	16 (4)
Growth from within	9 (18)	4 (27)	6 (27)	3 (8)	12 (46)	28 (26)	14 (33)	11 (38)	4 (24)	8 (29)	8 (33)	107 (27)
Selective growth thro.acquisitions	11 (22)	1 (7)	6 (27)	6 (15)	2 (8)	23 (21)	6 (14)	2 (7)	4 (23)	3 (11)	2 (8)	66 (17)
Selective Growth from within	22 (44)	7 (46)	8 (36)	18 (46)	11 (42)	46 (43)	18 (43)	13 (45)	6 (35)	13 (46)	11 (46)	173 (43)
Maintain operations/ generate cash flow	1 (2)	1 (7)	1 (5)	11 (28)	0 (0)	7 (6)	1 (2)	2 (7)	2 (12)	4 (14)	3 (13)	33 (8)
Shrinking operations	0 (0)	0 (0)	0 (0)	1 (3)	0 (0)	1 (1)	2 (5)	1 (3)	0 (0)	0 (0)	0 (0)	5 (1)
Total	50 (100)	15 (100)	22 (100)	39 (100)	26 (100)	108 (100)	42 (100)	29 (100)	17 (100)	28 (100)	24 (100)	400 (100)

The entries in each cell are "number of respondents" and ("column percentage") respectively.

Table 6
Rate of Change in Business Environment by Industry (Question 2)

Rate of change in business environment	Commercial Banks	Diversified Financial	Diversified Service	Hospitals	Life Insurance	Large Manu-facturing	Medium Manu-facturing	Retailers/ Wholesalers	Transporta-tion	Utilities	Miscella-neous	Total
Low (Score: 9 – 21)	1 (2)	4 (31)	7 (39)	12 (33)	5 (19)	22 (21)	7 (17)	12 (41)	6 (38)	13 (52)	8 (40)	97 (26)
Medium (Score: 22 – 27)	9 (19)	3 (23)	7 (39)	11 (31)	8 (31)	46 (44)	20 (49)	9 (31)	6 (37)	7 (28)	4 (20)	130 (35)
High (Score: 28 – 50)	37 (79)	6 (46)	4 (22)	13 (36)	13 (50)	36 (35)	14 (34)	8 (28)	4 (25)	5 (20)	8 (40)	148 (39)
Total	47 (100)	13 (100)	18 (100)	36 (100)	26 (100)	104 (100)	41 (100)	29 (100)	16 (100)	25 (100)	20 (100)	375 (100)

company transfers in 31% of the companies. Transfers account for 1% to 5% of the total sales in 43% of the firms. Intracompany transfers are relatively more popular in the manufacturing and retail industries.

OVERALL FINANCIAL PERFORMANCE

The respondents were asked to identify which of the following terms best described their overall financial performance: losing money, about breakeven, profitable but less so than comparable companies, or more profitable than comparable companies. Only 7% of the respondents state that they are losing money. Slightly over 50% of the firms rate themselves as being more profitable than comparable companies (Table 7, Question 4).

USE OF FORMAL BUDGET PROGRAMS AND PROFIT CENTERS

About 97% of the participants state that they have a formal budget program (Table 8, Question 5). This result is consistent with the findings of other recent studies discussed in chapter 1. Although 83% of the participating firms are subdivided into profit centers, there is a significant variation by industry on this dimension. Over 90% of the participants in commercial banking, diversified service, large manufacturing, and retail/wholesale industries use profit centers. However, only 27% of the hospitals, most of whom were operating on a not-for-profit basis, are adopting the profit center concept. Approximately 90% of the firms having a formal budget program used a 12-month budget period. The length of the budget period varied from 1 to 30 months. Three- and six-month budget periods were used by about 3% each of the responding companies.

The companies participating in the study seem to include many renowned firms in the surveyed industries (see Appendix II). No significant differences were found between the demographic characteristics of the respondents and those of the nonrespondents. Further, the survey was able to achieve a respectable response rate of about 40%. These data suggest that this study is based on a representative cross section of firms in the industries selected for the study.

Table 7
Overall Financial Performance by Industry (Question 4)

Overall financial performance	Commercial Banks	Diversified Financial	Diversified Service	Hospitals	Life Insurance	Large Manufacturing	Medium Manufacturing	Retailers/Wholesalers	Transportation	Utilities	Miscellaneous	Total
Losing money	0 (0)	1 (7)	2 (9)	6 (15)	0 (0)	7 (6)	7 (17)	2 (7)	2 (12)	0 (0)	2 (8)	29 (7)
About breakeven	1 (2)	2 (14)	0 (0)	16 (39)	1 (4)	4 (4)	1 (2)	1 (3)	0 (0)	0 (0)	0 (0)	26 (7)
Less profitable than comparable firms	17 (35)	2 (14)	6 (27)	4 (10)	11 (42)	39 (37)	10 (24)	12 (41)	4 (23)	15 (56)	6 (25)	126 (32)
More profitable than comparable firms	31 (63)	9 (65)	14 (64)	15 (36)	14 (54)	56 (53)	24 (57)	14 (49)	11 (65)	12 (44)	16 (67)	216 (54)
Total	49 (100)	14 (100)	22 (100)	41 (100)	26 (100)	106 (100)	42 (100)	29 (100)	17 (100)	27 (100)	24 (100)	397 (100)

The entries in each cell are "number of respondents" and ("column percentage") respectively.

Table 8
Use of Formal Budget Programs and Profit Centers by Industry (Questions 5 and 17)

Do you have a formal budget program?	Commercial Banks	Diversified Financial	Diversified Service	Hospitals	Life Insurance	Large Manufacturing	Medium Manufacturing	Retailers/ Wholesalers	Transportation	Utilities	Miscellaneous	Total
No	1 (2)	1 (7)	0 (0)	0 (0)	1 (4)	0 (0)	1 (2)	1 (3)	1 (6)	1 (4)	4 (17)	11 (3)
Yes	49 (98)	13 (93)	22 (100)	41 (100)	25 (96)	108 (100)	40 (98)	28 (97)	16 (94)	27 (96)	20 (83)	389 (97)
Is your company divided into profit centers? No	3 (6)	4 (29)	1 (5)	30 (73)	6 (23)	3 (3)	2 (5)	1 (3)	4 (24)	11 (39)	2 (8)	67 (17)
Yes	47 (94)	10 (71)	21 (95)	11 (27)	20 (77)	105 (97)	39 (95)	28 (97)	13 (76)	17 (61)	22 (92)	333 (83)
Total	50 (100	14 (100)	22 (100)	41 (100)	26 (100)	108 (100)	41 (100)	29 (100)	17 (100)	28 (100)	24 (100)	400 (100)

The entries in each cell are "number of respondents" and ("column percentage") respectively.

3

Management Philosophy and Budgeting

The top management of each company has specific beliefs about how the company ought to be managed and about the role of planning and control systems in managing various company activities. These beliefs are directly reflected in both the design and use of the planning and control system. Part II of the questionnaire (Questions 6 to 21) was used to collect data on the beliefs of the management of the participating firms. This chapter provides a summary of responses to Part II of the questionnaire, and the results are presented by industry.

INDIVIDUALS OR GROUPS INVOLVED IN FORMALLY APPROVING BUDGETS

The extent of involvement of senior managers and major corporate-level committees in approving budgets in a company is usually an indication of the importance attached to budgeting by the company. The specific individuals and committees involved in formally approving budgets are presented by industry in Table 9 (Question 6). The board of directors plays an active role in approving budgets in some service industries such as commercial banks, diversified services, hospitals, and transportation. However, the board plays a passive role in approving budgets in life insurance, medium manufacturing, and retail industries.

Other committees, including the executive committee, the management committee, the planning committee, and the budget committee, do not seem to play a decisive role in approving budgets in any of the industries. The involvement of the executive vice presidents and controllers is also quite low in formally approving budgets.

The key persons involved in formally approving budgets are the chairman of the board, the president, and the financial vice president. Of these three, the president is the most active, especially in the life insurance and medium manufacturing industries (Table 9). It is therefore clear that committees do not play a major role in approving budgets and that the senior corporate managers play a direct and active role during the budgetary process.

Only in 9% of the responding companies is the formal budget approval given by only one individual or committee. Two to six individuals or committees are involved in formally approving budgets in about 80% of the companies. Only 1% of the participants do not require any formal approval during the budgetary process. The use of multiple approvals and active involvement of senior managers suggests that in a typical company the top management considers budgeting to be an important process in managing the company activities.

THE PROCESS OF GOAL SETTING

Subordinate levels of management are requested to submit goals and objectives relating to their particular function for review and final approval by higher levels of management in about 72% of the responding firms (Table 10, Question 7). The bottom-up process is particularly popular (84%) in large manufacturing firms. The practice of establishing goals and objectives exclusively by members of higher management without consultation with subordinate levels of management is

Table 9
Individuals or Groups Involved in Formally Approving Budgets (Question 6)

Individual/Group	Commercial Banks	Diversified Financial	Diversified Service	Hospitals	Life Insurance	Large Manufacturing	Medium Manufacturing	Retailers/ Wholesalers	Transportation	Utilities	Miscellaneous	Total
Board of Directors	72	47	77	81	32	58	42	36	77	61	38	58
Executive Committee	32	33	36	54	24	28	17	21	6	39	10	29
Chairman of the Board	66	47	64	17	44	66	34	68	65	64	38	54
President	64	67	73	71	92	75	93	68	71	57	71	74
Executive Vice-President	42	27	46	42	48	38	34	32	35	46	43	39
Financial Vice-President	34	53	46	71	48	63	71	68	65	36	62	57
Controller	40	27	41	39	60	44	56	36	47	29	33	42
Management Committee	22	33	23	29	32	22	17	7	6	18	24	22
Planning Committee	16	13	14	7	12	6	10	0	12	7	0	8
Budget Committee	16	20	0	39	20	7	5	14	18	14	10	14
No. of Respondents	50	15	22	41	25	108	41	28	17	28	21	396

Unless otherwise stated, the entry in each cell indicates the percentage of firms in the industry where the individual/groups formally approve the budget.

Table 10
Goal-Setting Process Used by Industry (Question 7)

Goal Setting Process Used	Commercial Banks	Diversified Financial	Diversified Service	Hospitals	Life Insurance	Large Manufacturing	Medium Manufacturing	Retailers/ Wholesalers	Transportation	Utilities	Miscellaneous	Total
Goals and objectives are established exclusively by members of higher management without consultation with subordinate levels	1 (2)	1 (7)	1 (5)	5 (12)	1 (4)	3 (3)	1 (3)	6 (21)	2 (12)	2 (7)	2 (10)	25 (6)
Goals and objectives developed by higher levels of management and presented to subordinate levels for consideration and comments	14 (29)	5 (33)	5 (23)	9 (22)	6 (24)	12 (11)	11 (27)	5 (18)	0 (0)	3 (11)	4 (19)	74 (19)
Subordinate levels of management submit their goals and objectives for review and final approval by higher levels of management	30 (63)	8 (53)	15 (68)	27 (66)	18 (72)	91 (84)	28 (68)	16 (57)	14 (82)	23 (82)	13 (62)	283 (72)
Other	3 (6)	1 (7)	1 (4)	0 (0)	0 (0)	2 (2)	1 (2)	1 (4)	1 (6)	0 (0)	2 (9)	12 (3)
Total	48 (100)	15 (100)	22 (100)	41 (100)	25 (100)	108 (100)	41 (100)	28 (100)	17 (100)	28 (100)	21 (100)	394 (100)

The entries in each cell are "number of respondents" and ("column percentage") respectively.

uncommon, except in retail (21%), hospital (12%), and transportation (12%) industries. About 30% of the firms in the diversified finance and commercial banking industries develop goals and objectives at the senior management level and then present them to subordinate levels of management for consideration and comment prior to final adoption. Although the goals and objectives are usually developed using a bottom-up process in all industries, the practice is most popular in large manufacturing firms.

USE OF SPECIFIC NONFINANCIAL BUDGETARY TARGETS

The percentage of companies using various nonfinancial budgetary targets is presented by industry in Table 11 (Question 8). Productivity, quality of product or service, and new product/service development are the nonfinancial areas in which budgetary targets are usually established. Relationships with customers, employees attitudes, and public responsibility are areas chosen by less than 40% of the respondents for establishing budgetary targets. A vast majority of the firms (90%) use at least one nonfinancial target. Approximately 50% of the respondents use three to seven nonfinancial targets each. Over 20% of the firms in diversified finance, diversified service, manufacturing, and retail industries each use nine or more nonfinancial targets. The results suggest that most firms believe that both financial and nonfinancial targets should be established during the budgetary process and that the use of multiple targets is desirable.

EXTENT OF DIFFICULTY IN ACHIEVING THE FINANCIAL TARGETS USED IN BUDGETS

Companies differ in their beliefs about the extent to which budgetary targets should be difficult. The respondents were given five choices to indicate the level of difficulty of budgetary targets used in their companies: "almost impossible," " challenging," "slightly beyond reach," "just right," and "relatively easy." Budgetary targets are rated to be

Table 11
Percentage of Companies Using Specific Nonfinancial Targets by Industry (Question 8)

Non-Financial targets used	Commercial Banks	Diversified Financial	Diversified Service	Hospitals	Life Insurance	Large Manufacturing	Medium Manufacturing	Retailers/ Wholesalers	Transportation	Utilities	Miscellaneous	Total
New Product/ Service Department	76	79	57	31	84	66	67	46	35	30	60	59
Quality of Product/ Service	71	64	55	73	68	64	68	54	77	79	74	67
Market Share	60	43	59	21	32	67	49	54	53	30	53	51
Customer Relations	65	73	55	51	61	46	55	56	19	79	58	55
Relationships with Suppliers	14	27	38	21	14	37	47	35	6	40	56	32
Productivity	66	87	64	82	54	79	68	77	60	75	78	73
Human Resources Development	72	73	57	59	52	62	59	54	47	64	68	61
Employee Attitudes	33	50	36	56	26	35	41	46	31	41	39	39
Public Responsibility	41	36	36	54	38	40	26	28	25	67	39	40
Balance between Short- and long-range goals	55	42	59	43	41	60	55	36	29	46	67	52

Since a company could use more than one nonfinancial target, the percentages in each column do not add up to 100%.

"challenging," by nearly 52% of the respondents (Table 12, Question 9). Only 22% of the participants state that their financial targets are "just right," or "relatively easy." In other words, about 78% of the companies included in the study use financial targets that are "slightly beyond reach," "challenging," or "almost impossible."

Implicitly this suggests that senior managers in U.S. firms believe that the use of difficult financial targets is more desirable than the adoption of reasonable or easy targets. Medium manufacturing and diversified financial firms use stringent financial targets, while commercial banks, life insurance companies, retail firms, and transportation companies adopt more equitable financial targets. These results raise an ethical question: Are the firms subjecting their managers to an unacceptable level of budgetary pressure? Another relevant question is whether difficult targets do in fact lead to increased productivity.

USE OF BUDGETS FOR PLANNING, COORDINATION, AND EVALUATION

Nearly 75% of the respondents use the same budget for planning, coordination, and evaluation (Table 13, Question 10). About 13% of the participants use budgets only for planning and coordination. The remaining firms either prepared two budgets, one for planning and coordination and the other for evaluation, or they used budgets only for evaluation. Budget targets for planning and coordination need to be accurate, while those for evaluation should be perceived to be fair by the budgetees. Hence, the widespread practice of using the same budget for all purposes is undesirable and may decrease budgetary effectiveness.

Nearly one-third of the participants do not review their budgets either for planning or evaluation purposes (Tables 14, and 15, Question 10). Of the companies that review their budgets for planning purposes, monthly review seems to be the most popular frequency (42% of all firms). Semi-annual reviews of annual budgets for planning purposes are conducted by only 6% of the participating firms. Approximately 29% of the

Table 12
Extent of Difficulty in Achieving the Financial Targets Used in Budgets (Question 9)

Extent of difficulty	Commercial Banks	Diversified Financial	Diversified Service	Hospitals	Life Insurance	Large Manu-facturing	Medium Manu-facturing	Retailers/ Wholesalers	Transporta-tion	Utilities	Miscella-neous	Total
Almost impossible	0 (0)	0 (0)	1 (5)	3 (8)	0 (0)	7 (6)	9 (22)	2 (7)	3 (19)	2 (7)	1 (5)	28 (7)
Challenging	23 (47)	10 (71)	11 (50)	24 (60)	11 (46)	59 (55)	20 (49)	11 (39)	5 (31)	16 (57)	11 (52)	201 (52)
Slightly beyond reach	13 (27)	1 (7)	8 (36)	7 (17)	6 (25)	16 (15)	8 (20)	5 (18)	3 (19)	1 (4)	5 (24)	73 (19)
Just right	8 (16)	3 (22)	2 (9)	5 (13)	3 (12)	18 (17)	3 (7)	9 (32)	2 (12)	8 (29)	3 (14)	64 (16)
Relatively easy	5 (10)	0 (0)	0 (0)	1 (2)	4 (17)	7 (7)	1 (2)	1 (4)	3 (19)	1 (3)	1 (5)	24 (6)
Total	49 (100)	14 (100)	22 (100)	40 (100)	24 (100)	107 (100)	41 (100)	28 (100)	16 (100)	28 (100)	21 (100)	390 (100)

The entries in each cell are "number of respondents" and ("column percentage") respectively.

Table 13
Use of Budgets for Planning, Coordination, and Evaluation (Question 10)

Budget Usage Pattern	Commercial Banks	Diversified Financial	Diversified Service	Hospitals	Life Insurance	Large Manufacturing	Medium Manufacturing	Retailers/ Wholesalers	Transportation	Utilities	Miscellaneous	Total
Two separate budgets are used	3 (6)	0 (0)	3 (14)	0 (0)	2 (8)	6 (6)	4 (10)	4 (14)	2 (12)	3 (11)	1 (5)	28 (7)
Only one budget is prepared and it is used for planning, coordination and evaluation	38 (78)	12 (80)	16 (73)	34 (83)	17 (68)	89 (82)	29 (71)	18 (64)	10 (59)	17 (61)	14 (74)	294 (75)
Only one budget is prepared and it is used for evaluation purposes	3 (6)	1 (7)	2 (9)	3 (7)	1 (4)	2 (2)	3 (7)	0 (0)	1 (6)	4 (14)	1 (5)	21 (5)
Only one budget is prepared and it is used for planning and coordination purposes	5 (10)	2 (13)	1 (4)	4 (10)	5 (20)	11 (10)	5 (12)	6 (22)	4 (23)	4 (14)	3 (16)	50 (13)
Total	49 (100)	15 (100)	22 (100)	41 (100)	25 (100)	108 (100)	41 (100)	28 (100)	17 (100)	28 (100)	19 (100)	393 (100)

The entries in each cell are "number of respondents" and ("column percentage") respectively.

29

Table 14
Frequency of Review of Annual Budget for Planning Purposes (Question 10)

Frequency of Review	Commercial Banks	Diversified Financial	Diversified Service	Hospitals	Life Insurance	Large Manufacturing	Medium Manufacturing	Retailers/ Wholesalers	Transportation	Utilities	Miscella- neous	Total
Never reviewed	23 (49)	1 (8)	5 (23)	13 (35)	1 (4)	36 (34)	12 (30)	7 (26)	4 (23)	12 (45)	6 (30)	120 (32)
Monthly	16 (34)	5 (38)	7 (32)	11 (30)	11 (48)	50 (47)	17 (42)	12 (44)	7 (41)	12 (44)	10 (50)	158 (42)
Quarterly	3 (6)	3 (23)	1 (4)	8 (22)	3 (13)	8 (8)	6 (15)	8 (30)	3 (18)	3 (11)	3 (15)	49 (13)
Semi-annually	4 (9)	0 (0)	4 (18)	2 (5)	6 (26)	4 (4)	3 (8)	0 (0)	1 (6)	0 (0)	1 (5)	25 (6)
Other	1 (2)	4 (31)	5 (23)	3 (8)	2 (9)	8 (7)	2 (5)	0 (0)	2 (12)	0 (0)	0 (0)	27 (7)
Total	47 (100)	13 (100)	22 (100)	37 (100)	23 (100)	106 (100)	40 (100)	27 (100)	17 (100)	27 (100)	20 (100)	379 (100)

The entries in each cell are "number of respondents" and ("column percentage") respectively.

Table 15
Frequency of Review of Annual Budget for Evaluation Purposes (Question 10)

Frequency of Review	Commercial Banks	Diversified Financial	Diversified Service	Hospitals	Life Insurance	Large Manu-facturing	Medium Manu-facturing	Retailers/ Wholesalers	Transporta-tion	Utilities	Miscella-neous	Total
Never reviewed	18 (39)	5 (34)	7 (32)	23 (56)	3 (14)	29 (29)	9 (26)	12 (48)	4 (27)	9 (33)	6 (32)	125 (34)
Monthly	11 (24)	4 (27)	5 (23)	10 (24)	10 (48)	33 (33)	14 (40)	5 (20)	2 (13)	6 (22)	5 (26)	105 (29)
Quarterly	4 (9)	1 (6)	3 (14)	2 (5)	3 (14)	10 (10)	8 (23)	2 (8)	3 (20)	3 (11)	4 (21)	43 (12)
Semi-annually	12 (26)	0 (0)	3 (13)	4 (10)	2 (10)	18 (18)	4 (11)	5 (20)	4 (27)	4 (15)	3 (16)	59 (16)
Other	1 (2)	5 (33)	4 (18)	2 (5)	3 (14)	10 (10)	0 (0)	1 (4)	2 (13)	5 (19)	1 (5)	34 (9)
Total	46 (100)	15 (100)	22 (100)	41 (100)	21 (100)	100 (100)	35 (100)	25 (100)	15 (100)	27 (100)	19 (100)	366 (100)

The entries in each cell are "number of respondents" and ("column percentage") respectively.

participating companies review their annual budgets monthly for evaluation purposes. Semi-annual reviews of budgets for evaluation purposes are used by about 16% of the participants.

About 45% of the firms in the commercial banking and utility industries never review their budgets for planning. Nearly half the firms in the hospital and retail sectors do not review their budgets for evaluation. Life insurance firms are the most active reviewers, and nearly half the firms in the industry review their annual budgets on a monthly basis both for planning and evaluation. Thus, the importance assigned to review of budgets, either for planning or for evaluation, varies significantly across industries.

USE OF QUANTITATIVE DATA IN ASSESSING AND EVALUATING ORGANIZATIONAL SUBUNITS

Higher-level managers have varying preferences for the use of quantitative information. Approximately 53% of the participants give more importance to quantitative data in evaluating organizational subunits, while 26% of the firms focus almost equally on quantitative and qualitative data (Table 16, Question 11). Only 10% of the respondents give more importance to qualitative information for evaluation purposes. Commercial banks, hospitals, and utility companies are slightly less quantitatively oriented than the other industries. Senior managers in most firms therefore seem to believe that quantitative information should be given more importance than qualitative data.

USE OF COMPUTERS IN BUDGETING

Almost all companies use their computers for preparing budgets (96%) and performance reports (90%). Preparation of long-range forecasts and financial plans using computers is less frequent and is practiced by about three-fourths of the participants (Table 17, Question 12). Computer-based analysis of economic data is the least frequent (57%) use of computers in budgeting, while the application of computers for budget preparation is the most frequent use (96%). In general, hospitals, medium manufacturing firms, and retail companies use compu-

Table 16

Use of Quantitative Data by Higher-Level Managers for Evaluating Organizational Subunits (Question 11)

Type of data preferred by senior managers	Commercial Banks	Diversified Financial	Diversified Service	Hospitals	Life Insurance	Large Manufacturing	Medium Manufacturing	Retailers/ Wholesalers	Transportation	Utilities	Miscellaneous	Total
They seem to focus primarily on quantitative data	5 (10)	2 (13)	4 (18)	5 (12)	5 (20)	10 (9)	4 (10)	2 (7)	1 (6)	2 (7)	2 (10)	42 (11)
While they focus on both quantitative and qualitative data, more importance is given to quantitative data	26 (53)	9 (60)	14 (64)	17 (42)	13 (52)	55 (52)	25 (61)	17 (61)	13 (76)	11 (39)	8 (38)	208 (53)
They seem to focus almost equally on quantitative and qualitative data	8 (16)	3 (20)	3 (14)	14 (34)	4 (16)	35 (33)	9 (22)	4 (14)	2 (12)	12 (43)	8 (38)	102 (26)
While they focus on both quantitative and qualitative data more importance is given to qualitative data.	9 (19)	1 (7)	1 (4)	5 (12)	3 (12)	7 (6)	1 (2)	4 (14)	1 (6)	3 (11)	3 (14)	38 (9)
They seem to focus primarily on qualitative data	1 (2)	0 (0)	0 (0)	0 (0)	0 (0)	0 (0)	2 (5)	1 (4)	0 (0)	0 (0)	0 (0)	4 (1)
Total	49 (100)	15 (100)	22 (100)	41 (100)	25 (100)	107 (100)	4i (100)	28 (100)	17 (100)	28 (100)	21 (100)	394 (100)

The entries in each cell are "number of respondents" and ("column percentage") respectively.

Table 17
Use of Computers for Specific Planning and Control Purposes by Industry (Question 12)

Percentage of firms using computers for	Commercial Banks	Diversified Financial	Diversified Service	Hospitals	Life Insurance	Large Manufacturing	Medium Manufacturing	Retailers/ Wholesalers	Transportation	Utilities	Miscellaneous	Total
Analysis of economic data	58	60	64	45	50	65	32	39	65	96	50	57
Preparation of long-range forecasts	71	93	68	59	79	86	61	56	65	100	67	74
Preparation of long-range financial plans	75	87	91	66	76	91	68	57	77	100	71	79
Preparation of Budgets	98	100	100	95	92	97	90	96	100	96	91	96
Preparation of performance reports	92	100	86	88	84	94	85	89	94	93	81	90
Number of Respondents	48	15	22	41	25	108	41	28	17	28	21	394

All numbers are percentages unless otherwise specified.

ters less frequently, while almost all diversified finance, large manufacturing, and utility firms use computers for preparing long-range plans and budgets. These results suggest that most firms use computers in preparing budgets and performance reports.

USE OF BUDGETS BY HIGHER-LEVEL MANAGERS FOR VARIOUS PURPOSES

Budgets are used for planning purposes to a moderate extent by 32% of the participants and to a great extent by 51%. Hospitals, life insurance firms, and utilities use budgets to a relatively small extent for this purpose.

Budgets are used for coordinating various activities to a moderate extent in 34% of the firms and to a great extent in 24% of the firms. Diversified services, hospitals, and life insurance firms use budgets to a lesser extent for coordinating various activities.

Use of budgets for motivational purposes is practiced to a moderate extent by 33% of the respondents and to a great extent by 35%. Motivational use of budgets is particularly emphasized by firms in commercial banking, diversified service, hospitals, manufacturing, and retail industries.

Nearly three-fourths of the respondents use budgets either to a moderate or great extent for evaluating the performance of managers. Commercial banks and large manufacturing firms rely heavily on budgets in evaluating managers, while transportation and utilities industries place a lesser emphasis on budgets for this purpose.

Budgets are used for determining managerial compensation to the greatest extent in large manufacturing firms and to the least extent in hospitals and life insurance companies. About 22% of the respondents report that they use budgets to a moderate extent for compensating managers, and 32% state that they use budgets to a great extent for that purpose.

Only 29% of the respondents use budgets to a moderate or great extent for educating and developing managers. Diversified service and life insurance companies emphasize this use the least. These results suggest that companies tend to focus on the use of budgets for getting the job done and may not emphasize the use of budgets for educating and developing managers. Budgets could help managers in identifying more effective approaches to planning, implementing the plans, monitoring the progress against plans, and finally reviewing the appropriateness of plan targets and the process by which the plans were implemented. This approach to educating and developing managers has not been explored sufficiently by most companies. The focus is on the tangible and operational uses of budgeting.

About 70% of the respondents consider budgets to be an important device for communicating the priorities established by the top management. Diversified financial firms, commercial banks, and life insurance companies give more emphasis to this use of budgets.

Nearly 90% of the participants use budgets for determining managerial compensation, as well as for educating and developing managers. Over 95% of the respondents use budgets to varying degrees for each of the other five uses. The weighted average score of the importance (1 = used to a limited extent to 5 = used to a great extent) for different uses of budgets are as follows (Table 18, Question 13):

Coordinating various activities	4.3
Planning	4.0
Evaluating managers	3.9
Communicating the priorities established by the top management	3.9
Motivating managers	3.7
Compensating managers	3.6
Educating and developing managers	2.9

In summary, most firms use budgets for multiple purposes. Planning and coordination uses of budgets are emphasized the most, while educational and developmental uses of budgets receive the least attention.

The extent to which budgets are used for various purposes is reflected in the total score for various uses of budgets (Table 19, Question 13). Commercial banks, diversified financial

Table 18
Relative Importance Assigned by Higher-Level Managers to Alternative Uses of Budgets
(Question 13)

Alternative Uses of Budgets	Commercial Banks	Diversified Financial	Diversified Service	Hospitals	Life Insurance	Large Manufacturing	Medium Manufacturing	Retailers/ Wholesalers	Transportation	Utilities	Miscellaneous	Total
Planning	4.0	4.4	4.0	3.5	3.8	4.3	3.5	3.4	4.0	4.9	3.8	4.0
Coordinating various activities	4.2	4.3	4.1	3.9	4.3	4.5	4.3	4.5	4.2	4.4	4.0	4.3
Motivating Managers	3.8	4.0	3.4	3.4	3.3	3.8	3.8	3.8	3.7	4.1	3.9	3.7
Evaluating Managers	3.8	4.2	3.9	3.7	3.5	4.1	3.9	3.9	3.6	3.6	3.7	3.9
Compensating Managers	3.2	4.2	3.7	3.0	2.8	4.1	3.9	3.4	3.7	3.1	3.3	3.6
Educating and Developing Managers	2.8	3.2	2.8	3.0	2.4	3.1	2.9	2.9	2.7	3.0	2.7	2.9
Communicating the priorities established by top management	4.1	4.4	3.8	3.6	4.0	4.0	4.0	3.9	3.8	4.2	3.6	3.9

The entries in each cell represent average ratings of importance on a five-point scale with
1 = not used to 5 = used to a great extent.

Table 19
Total Score on Use of Budgets for Various Purposes (Question 13)

Total Score	Commercial Banks	Diversified Financial	Diversified Service	Hospitals	Life Insurance	Large Manu- facturing	Medium Manu- facturing	Retailers/ Wholesalers	Transporta- tion	Utilities	Miscella- neous	Total
≤ 20	5 (10)	3 (23)	4 (18)	12 (30)	7 (29)	18 (17)	6 (15)	6 (22)	6 (35)	5 (18)	4 (20)	76 (20)
21 – 25	10 (21)	2 (15)	8 (36)	12 (30)	10 (42)	14 (13)	12 (30)	5 (19)	2 (12)	10 (36)	7 (35)	92 (24)
26 – 30	22 (46)	4 (31)	7 (32)	11 (27)	6 (25)	50 (47)	9 (22)	10 (37)	4 (24)	8 (28)	6 (30)	137 (35)
31 – 35	11 (23)	4 (31)	3 (14)	5 (13)	1 (4)	25 (23)	13 (33)	6 (22)	5 (29)	5 (18)	3 (15)	81 (21)
Total	48 (100)	13 (100)	22 (100)	40 (100)	24 (100)	107 (100)	40 (100)	27 (100)	17 (100)	28 (100)	20 (100)	386 (100)

The total score is the algebraic sum of the scores on seven different uses, and a five-point scale is used so that the total score has a range of 7 to 35.

companies, and large manufacturing firms are heavy users of budgets; medium manufacturing and retailers/wholesalers are medium users; and diversified services, hospitals, life insurers, transportation, and utilities are selective users of budgets. This suggests that some industries can benefit from selective adoption of budgetary practices used in other industries.

TOP MANAGEMENT VIEW OF BUDGETS

Nearly 60% of the respondents stated that the top management in their companies believe that budgets provided a tool which could be used to motivate subordinates to increase output and improve efficiency through managerial planning and control (Table 20, Question 14). Approximately 13% of the participants describe their top management's view of budgets in each of these ways:

1. Budgets improve efficiency and output by effectively exerting pressure on subordinates.
2. Although budgets motivate subordinates, they primarily improve efficiency and output through pressure on subordinates.
3. Although budgets exert some pressure on subordinates, they primarily increase efficiency and output through motivation of employees.

Most firms use budgets to motivate people as well as to improve efficiency. However, 26% of the firms use budgets to exert pressure on subordinates so that efficiency and output would improve.

PROPORTION OF HIGHER-LEVEL CORPORATE MANAGERS WITH A FINANCIAL BACKGROUND

The proportion of firms with no financial expertise at the senior management level is less than 1%. Over 53% of the firms have 1% to 20% of the higher-level managers with a financial background. Commercial banks and diversified service firms have the largest proportion (over 40%) of companies with 41% or more of the higher-level corporate managers having financial education or experience.

Table 20
Top Management View of Budgets as Control Devices (Question 14)

Top Management view of Budgets	Commercial Banks	Diversified Financial	Diversified Service	Hospitals	Life Insurance	Large Manu-facturing	Medium Manu-facturing	Retailers/ Wholesalers	Transporta-tion	Utilities	Miscellaneous	Total
Budgets can be used effectively to exert pressure on subordinates thereby improving efficiency and output	5 (11)	3 (20)	1 (5)	4 (10)	4 (17)	17 (16)	5 (13)	5 (18)	2 (12)	3 (11)	0 (0)	49 (12)
Budgets should be used to motivate subordinates to increase output and improve efficiency through participation in managerial planning and control	28 (60)	7 (47)	15 (71)	26 (63)	10 (42)	62 (59)	25 (62)	11 (39)	11 (69)	20 (71)	16 (80)	231 (60)
Budgets do motivate subordinates but primarily increase efficiency and outout through pressure on subordinates	9 (19)	2 (13)	2 (10)	2 (5)	6 (25)	13 (12)	5 (13)	8 (29)	0 (0)	4 (14)	2 (10)	53 (14)
Budgets do exert some pressure on subordinates but primarily increase efficiency through motivation of employees	5 (10)	3 (20)	3 (14)	9 (22)	4 (16)	14 (13)	5 (12)	4 (14)	3 (19)	1 (4)	2 (10)	53 (14)
Total	47 (100)	15 (100)	21 (100)	41 (100)	24 (100)	106 (100)	40 (100)	28 (100)	16 (100)	28 (100)	20 (100)	386 (100)

The entries in each cell are "number of respondents" and ("column percentage") respectively.

The frequency distribution of respondents by industry and size of the corporate budget department is presented in Table 21 (Question 15). Approximately 25% of the firms have a budget department with one or two persons, and over 50% of the participants have a staff of fewer than seven persons in their budget department. The remaining firms have a budget department with 7 to 200 persons. The wide variation in the size of the budget department in nearly half the firms is worth noting and suggests that there may be substantial differences among firms in their respective expectation of the budget department and their assessment of the resources needed to run the department.

FREQUENCY OF FORMAL BUDGET MEETINGS OF CORPORATE MANAGERS WITH LOWER-LEVEL MANAGERS

Corporate managers who desire active participation in the activities of managers at lower levels would prefer more frequent formal meetings. As Table 22 (Question 16) suggests, nearly half the companies prefer monthly meetings of corporate managers with lower-level managers, and in about 30% of the participating firms, corporate managers meet with divisional managers on a quarterly basis. Thus, in nearly 80% of the firms, corporate and divisional managers interact in formal meetings at least once each quarter. Formal budget meetings of corporate and divisional managers are held only once a year in about 15% of transportation and utility firms. Monthly meetings are most popular in hospitals (65%) and medium manufacturing companies (68%).

LOCATION OF PROFIT CENTERS BY INDUSTRY

Hospitals and life insurance firms have a relatively low level of geographical dispersion within the United States. More than half of the participants from manufacturing, commercial banking, and transportation industries have profit centers outside the United States.

The average number of profit centers per firm by location is presented in Table 23 (Question 17). Commercial banks and

Table 21
Size of Corporate Budget Department by Industry (Question 15)

No. of employees in Corp. Budget Dept.	Commercial Banks	Diversified Financial	Diversified Service	Hospitals	Life Insurance	Large Manufacturing	Medium Manufacturing	Retailers/ Wholesalers	Transportation	Utilities	Miscellaneous	Total
0–2	6 (15)	0 (0)	8 (45)	16 (53)	2 (14)	14 (18)	12 (35)	10 (45)	3 (23)	0 (0)	5 (38)	76 (26)
3 – 6	15 (38)	5 (56)	4 (22)	11 (37)	5 (33)	27 (34)	20 (59)	8 (36)	5 (38)	6 (35)	6 (46)	112 (39)
7 – 10	11 (27)	2 (22)	1 (6)	1 (4)	2 (13)	18 (23)	1 (3)	1 (5)	2 (16)	2 (12)	1 (8)	42 (15)
11 – 20	5 (13)	0 (0)	1 (5)	0 (0)	3 (20)	12 (15)	0 (0)	1 (5)	2 (15)	3 (18)	0 (0)	27 (9)
21 – 30	2 (5)	1 (11)	1 (6)	1 (3)	2 (13)	3 (4)	0 (0)	0 (0)	1 (8)	3 (18)	1 (8)	15 (5)
31 – 50	0 (0)	0 (0)	2 (11)	1 (3)	0 (0)	2 (2)	1 (3)	0 (0)	0 (0)	0 (0)	0 (0)	6 (2)
51 – 100	0 (0)	0 (0)	1 (5)	0 (0)	0 (0)	3 (3)	0 (0)	2 (9)	0 (0)	3 (17)	0 (0)	9 (3)
101 – 200	1 (2)	1 (11)	0 (0)	0 (0)	1 (7)	1 (1)	0 (0)	0 (0)	0 (0)	0 (0)	0 (0)	4 (1)
Total	40 (100)	9 (100)	18 (100)	30 (100)	15 (100)	80 (100)	34 (100)	22 (100)	13 (100)	17 (100)	13 (100)	291 (100)

The entries in each cell are "number of respondents" and ("column percentage") respectively.

Table 22
Frequency of Formal Budget Meetings between Corporate and Lower-Level Managers (Question 16)

Frequency	Commercial Banks	Diversified Financial	Diversified Service	Hospitals	Life Insurance	Large Manufacturing	Medium Manufacturing	Retailers/ Wholesalers	Transportation	Utilities	Miscellaneous	Total
Weekly	1 (2)	0 (0)	0 (0)	0 (0)	0 (0)	3 (3)	0 (0)	1 (3)	0 (0)	1 (3)	0 (0)	6 (2)
Monthly	22 (46)	6 (40)	10 (45)	26 (65)	4 (17)	49 (46)	28 (68)	13 (46)	6 (35)	9 (32)	7 (33)	180 (46)
Quarterly	16 (33)	6 (40)	6 (27)	8 (20)	11 (46)	29 (27)	12 (29)	7 (25)	5 (29)	8 (29)	6 (29)	114 (29)
Semiannually	2 (4)	1 (7)	1 (5)	1 (3)	3 (12)	10 (9)	0 (0)	5 (18)	2 (12)	3 (11)	2 (10)	30 (8)
Annually	5 (11)	0 (0)	3 (14)	5 (12)	1 (4)	12 (11)	0 (0)	1 (4)	3 (18)	4 (14)	2 (9)	36 (9)
Other	2 (4)	2 (13)	2 (9)	0 (0)	5 (21)	4 (4)	1 (3)	1 (4)	1 (6)	3 (11)	4 (19)	25 (6)
Total	48 (100)	15 (100)	22 (100)	40 (100)	24 (100)	107 (100)	41 (100)	28 (100)	17 (100)	28 (100)	21 (100)	391 (100)

The entries in each cell are "number of respondents" and ("column percentage") respectively.

transportation firms have the highest number of profit centers per firm, followed by diversified financial and retailers/wholesalers. Commercial banks, diversified financial, and retail firms have a relatively larger number of domestic profit centers more than 50 miles away from corporate headquarters. Transportation, diversified financial, and large manufacturing firms have more profit centers abroad. Diversified service firms, hospitals, life insurance companies, medium manufacturers, and utilities have the least number of profit centers, either within the United States or overseas (Table 23).

EXTENT OF VARIATION IN BUDGET POLICIES AND PROCEDURES ACROSS PROFIT CENTERS

Retailers and bankers report the least amount of variation in budget policies and procedures across their profit centers (Table 24, Question 18). This could mean that both these industries have a high degree of similarity among their profit centers so that standardized budgetary controls are feasible. Transportation, life insurance, diversified service, and utilities state that there are substantial variations in budget practices among their profit centers. Firms reporting greater variation in budget policies and procedures in these industries probably believe that the increased cost and difficulty of using heterogeneous controls was less than the incremental benefits of such customized controls. Usually, the presence of diversity among profit centers is associated with variations in budget practices.

PERCENTAGE OF FIRMS HAVING MANAGERS OR GROUPS WITH SPECIFIC TITLES AT THE PROFIT CENTER LEVEL

Budget and long-range planning committees are used mostly in hospitals and utilities (Table 25, Question 19). Committees at the profit center level are not popular in other industries. Each profit center has a controller in over three-fourths of the participating firms. Over 90% of the respondents from large manufacturing

Table 23
Average Number of Profit Centers per Firm by Location and by Industry (Question 17)

Average number of profit centers/firm	Commercial Banks	Diversified Financial	Diversified Service	Hospitals	Life Insurance	Large Manufacturing	Medium Manufacturing	Retailers/ Wholesalers	Transportation	Utilities	Miscellaneous	Total
Within 50 miles of Corporate headquarters in the U.S.	35.3	8.7	4.4	13.9	9.4	7.7	3.7	13.5	12.2	12.9	11.2	12.5
More than 50 miles away from corporate headquarters in the U.S.	28.4	28.0	12.2	14.9	22.0	15.0	4.6	26.4	22.4	8.5	5.5	15.7
Outside the U.S.	7.0	12.0	2.5	3.9	6.0	11.5	4.7	6.4	27.1	1.1	5.7	8.7
Total	70.7	48.7	19.1	32.7	37.4	34.2	13.0	46.3	61.7	22.5	22.4	36.9

The average numbers were computed by dividing the total number of profit centers in each type of location by the number of firms having profit centers at the location. Within each industry, the number of firms having profit centers at each type of location could vary. Hence the numbers in the table should be added vertically.

Table 24
Extent of Variation in Budget Policies and Procedures across Profit Centers (Question 18)

Extent of Variation	Commercial Banks	Diversified Financial	Diversified Service	Hospitals	Life Insurance	Large Manufacturing	Medium Manufacturing	Retailers/ Wholesalers	Transportation	Utilities	Miscellaneous	Total
Budgets are not used in profit centers	0 (0)	0 (0)	0 (0)	0 (0)	2 (11)	1 (1)	0 (0)	1 (4)	0 (0)	0 (0)	1 (5)	5 (1)
No variation	18 (40)	2 (18)	5 (24)	4 (45)	4 (22)	33 (32)	17 (45)	16 (59)	2 (15)	4 (25)	7 (37)	112 (35)
Slight Variation	21 (47)	6 (55)	8 (38)	2 (22)	5 (28)	37 (35)	12 (32)	7 (26)	4 (31)	6 (38)	6 (32)	114 (35)
Moderate Variation	3 (7)	1 (9)	5 (24)	2 (22)	5 (28)	19 (18)	5 (13)	1 (4)	7 (54)	5 (31)	4 (21)	57 (18)
Considerable Variation	3 (6)	2 (18)	1 (5)	0 (0)	2 (11)	6 (6)	2 (5)	1 (3)	0 (0)	0 (0)	1 (5)	18 (6)
Each profit center has its own policies and procedures	0 (0)	0 (0)	2 (9)	1 (11)	0 (0)	8 (8)	2 (5)	1 (4)	0 (0)	1 (6)	0 (0)	15 (5)
Total	45 (100)	11 (100)	21 (100)	9 (100)	18 (100)	104 (100)	38 (100)	27 (100)	13 (100)	16 (100)	19 (100)	321 (100)

The entries in each cell are "number of respondents" and ("column percentage") respectively.

Table 25
Percentage of Firms Having Managers or Groups with Selected Titles at the Profit Center Level (Question 19)

Title of Manager or Group	Commercial Banks	Diversified Financial	Diversified Service	Hospitals	Life Insurance	Large Manu- facturing	Medium Manu- facturing	Retailers/ Wholesalers	Transporta- tion	Utilities	Miscella- neous	Total
Controller	52	64	91	56	35	96	79	63	85	75	74	76
Budget Manager	45	27	52	38	35	56	23	23	39	81	41	45
Long-Range Planning Committee	14	9	20	50	19	15	14	12	8	38	38	18
Budget Committee	12	9	10	29	19	9	5	15	0	40	13	12
Internal Audit Manager	37	10	29	50	24	20	14	31	8	33	27	25
Planning Manager	25	46	38	70	39	53	19	8	39	75	35	40
Industrial Engineer	3	10	29	38	0	75	78	15	8	40	47	44
Standards Dept.	5	9	15	13	6	51	56	15	15	33	39	32

and diversified service industries report that they have a controller in their profit centers. Budget or planning managers are found in about 40% of the firms. Over half of the large manufacturers and utilities have a budget manager and/or a planning manager. Industrial engineers and standards departments are found mostly in the profit centers of manufacturing firms. Internal audit managers at the profit center level are reported by only 25% of the firms. Large manufacturing, utilities, and diversified services have more managers/committees with budget responsibilities at their profit center level, and life insurance firms have the least number of such managers or groups.

USE OF COMPUTERS FOR BUDGET-RELATED PURPOSES AT THE PROFIT CENTER LEVEL

Computers are used for budget-related purposes at the profit center level in nearly 90% of the participating firms. Nearly all of the firms in diversified service, utilities, and large manufacturing industries use computers in their profit centers, while only 70% each in diversified financial and hospitals adopted such a practice.

Of the firms using computers at the profit center level, profit centers in nearly 80% of the firms have direct access to their data base (Table 26, Question 20). Accessibility of data base to profit centers is the greatest in diversified service, diversified financial, and large manufacturing firms, and the least in commercial banking and retail sectors.

Corporate managers have direct access to the data base in 40% of the firms. The location where the profit center performance report is prepared varies across industries. The performance report is prepared at the corporate office in 93% of the commercial banks, 62% of diversified financial firms, 71% of hospitals, and 59% of retailers. Information systems are centralized in these industries. Profit centers prepare performance reports in 71% of diversified service and 74% of medium manufacturing firms. Both these industries seem to believe in decentralizing financial information systems. Computers at the corporate and divisional levels are compatible

Table 26

Percentage of Respondents Adopting Specific Practices in Using Computers for Budgeting at their Profit Center Level (Question 20)

Practice Used	Commercial Banks	Diversified Financial	Diversified Service	Hospitals	Life Insurance	Large Manufacturing	Medium Manufacturing	Retailers/ Wholesalers	Transportation	Utilities	Miscellaneous	Total
Profit centers has access to its data base	53	88	90	71	73	88	82	57	75	81	65	78
Corporate Managers have access to profit center data base	48	38	33	57	53	35	44	35	41	50	38	40
Location where profit center performance report is prepared:												
- Corporate office	93	62	29	71	53	44	26	59	36	44	47	49
- Profit center	7	25	71	29	47	54	74	41	55	56	53	50
- Not prepared	–	13	–	–	–	2	–	0	9	0	–	1
Computers at Corporate and divisional levels are compatible	86	100	70	71	93	72	70	86	91	93	72	78

in nearly 80% of the firms. Although computers are used at the profit center level for budgeting in over 85% of the firms, there seems to be a wide variation in top management philosophy about the extent to which financial information systems should be decentralized.

Diversified service and medium-sized manufacturing firms report highest levels of decentralization, while commercial banks and retailers have highly centralized financial information systems. It is worth noting that diversified service and medium-sized manufacturing firms also report low compatibility between corporate and divisional levels. Senior corporate managers need to examine whether the low level of compatibility between corporate and divisional computers is used by divisional managers as a conscious strategy to achieve a higher degree of autonomy. Other possible explanations for using incompatible computers could include differences in the computers used by newly acquired divisions and absence of a corporate policy or plan for management information systems. However, intentional creation of low compatibility between corporate and divisional computers leads to ineffective use of resources and should therefore be prevented.

RELATIVE IMPORTANCE PLACED BY TOP MANAGEMENT ON VARIOUS ORGANIZATIONAL DEVICES TO MANAGE CORPORATE-PROFIT CENTER RELATIONSHIPS

Annual budgeting system is rated as the most important organizational device to manage corporate-profit center relationships (Table 27, Question 21). Capital budgeting and informal contacts between corporate and profit center managers are respectively rated as the next two devices in importance. Capital budgets are rated high in all industries, except the financial services sector. Divisional, interdivisional, and corporate task forces and committees are rated as the least important. The low average scores received by formal goal setting, performance evaluation and compensation systems, and monthly budget reviews are surprising. Perhaps the difficulties associated with optimal design of goal-setting, evaluation, or compensation systems could lead to their low perceived importance. The ratings of long-range planning systems and monthly narrative reports are also quite low. Corporate top management therefore relies heavily on the annual budgeting system to manage the corporate-profit center relationships.

Approximately 90% of the respondents use 9 of the 12 organizational devices to manage their firms. Half of all participating firms use all 13 organizational devices (Table 28, Question 21). However, only annual budgets and capital expenditure approval systems receive significantly higher ratings for their relative importance. The use of a large number of organizational devices suggests that few firms are really satisfied with the way they manage corporate–profit center relationships and have therefore resorted to the use of more devices with the hope that the additional organizational devices used will improve the overall effectiveness of their control system. However, the presence of too many organizational devices may decrease the amount of attention that top management gives to each device.

SOME IMPORTANT ELEMENTS OF MANAGEMENT PHILOSOPHY

Top management philosophy is the guiding force behind the design and use of budgetary controls in any organization. This survey reveals that there are some relatively popular elements of management philosophy which reflect the views or assumptions of senior managers about how their respective firms should be managed. These beliefs (with appropriate table and question references) are summarized here:

- Multiple approvals for budgets are desirable (Question 6).
- A bottom-up goal-setting process is more effective than a top-down goal setting process (Table 10, Question 7).
- Both financial and nonfinancial targets should be used (Table 11, Question 8).
- Financial targets should be difficult in order to be effective (Table 12, Question 9).
- Budgets used for planning and coordination can also be used for evaluation (Table 13, Question 10).

Table 27

Relative Importance Placed by Corporate Top Management on Various Organizational Devices to Manage Corporate-Profit Center Relationships (Question 21)

Organizational Device	Commercial Banks	Diversified Financial	Diversified Service	Hospitals	Life Insurance	Large Manufacturing	Medium Manufacturing	Retailers/ Wholesalers	Transportation	Utilities	Miscellaneous	Total
Annual Budgeting System	4.1	4.1	3.9	4.1	3.9	4.4	4.1	3.6	4.5	4.7	3.8	4.2
Long-range planning system	2.5	3.2	2.9	2.8	3.0	3.6	3.1	2.0	3.1	3.8	2.6	3.1
Approval system for capital expenditures	3.4	3.0	4.0	4.1	2.7	4.3	4.2	4.1	3.8	4.6	4.1	4.0
Monthly narrative reports	2.3	3.4	3.4	3.0	1.9	3.5	3.2	2.6	3.3	3.4	2.9	3.1
Formal goal-setting system	3.3	3.7	3.1	2.5	3.2	3.6	3.6	2.8	3.4	3.8	3.2	3.4
Performance evaluation and compensation systems for budget center managers	3.5	4.0	3.6	2.2	3.2	4.0	3.8	3.3	3.2	3.1	3.4	3.6
Direct informal contacts between corporate and profit center managers	3.3	4.1	3.6	3.1	3.7	3.9	4.3	3.6	2.9	3.6	3.4	3.7

Interdivisional task forces and committees	2.5	2.8	1.9	2.9	2.4	2.0	1.9	1.1	1.4	2.3	1.4	2.0
Corporate and divisional task forces and committees	2.7	3.1	2.0	2.5	2.4	2.2	2.4	1.4	2.5	2.7	1.8	2.3
Group or operating VPs	3.1	3.5	3.8	2.7	3.4	4.2	3.3	3.0	2.8	2.8	3.1	3.5
Other full time employees responsible for interdivisional coordination	2.5	3.2	2.1	2.5	1.9	2.3	2.0	1.5	1.8	2.2	1.8	2.2
Planned interdivisional and corporate-divisional transfers of managers	1.6	2.7	1.6	1.4	1.4	2.2	1.6	1.3	1.6	2.1	1.4	1.8
Monthly budget review	3.0	3.1	3.2	3.5	1.9	3.0	3.6	3.2	3.0	3.6	3.3	3.1

The scores are based on a five-point scale (1 = of limited importance to 5 = of extreme importance)

Table 28
Number of Coordination Devices Used to Manage Corporate–Profit Center Relationships (Question 21)

No. of coordination devices used	Commercial Banks	Diversified Financial	Diversified Service	Hospitals	Life Insurance	Large Manufacturing	Medium Manufacturing	Retailers/ Wholesalers	Transportation	Utilities	Miscellaneous	Total
9 or less	6 (13)	0 (0)	2 (9)	3 (30)	3 (17)	7 (6)	2 (6)	11 (41)	4 (31)	3 (17)	3 (15)	44 (13)
10	4 (9)	0 (0)	1 (5)	0 (0)	3 (17)	10 (10)	6 (15)	3 (11)	3 (23)	0 (0)	2 (11)	32 (10)
11	3 (6)	2 (18)	3 (14)	2 (20)	4 (22)	5 (5)	4 (10)	1 (4)	2 (15)	4 (24)	0 (0)	30 (9)
12	11 (24)	1 (9)	5 (24)	1 (10)	2 (11)	17 (16)	11 (28)	2 (7)	1 (8)	2 (12)	4 (21)	57 (18)
13	22 (48)	8 (73)	10 (48)	4 (40)	6 (33)	65 (63)	16 (41)	10 (37)	3 (23)	8 (47)	10 (53)	162 (50)
Total	46 (100)	11 (100)	21 (100)	10 (100)	18 (100)	104 (100)	39 (100)	27 (100)	13 (100)	17 (100)	19 (100)	325 (100)

The entries in each cell are "number of respondents" and ("column percentage") respectively.

- It is appropriate to review budgets for possible revision of goals for planning and coordination, but not for evaluation purposes (Tables 14 and 15, Question 10).

- Both quantitative and qualitative data should be used in evaluating organizational subunits. However, more importance should be given to quantitative data (Table 16, Questions 11).

- It is important to emphasize the use of computers for various budget-related purposes, especially preparation of budgets and performance reports (Table 17, Question 12).

- Budgets should serve several purposes. The relative importance of various uses, in decreasing order, are coordinating various activities, planning, evaluating the managers, communicating the priorities established by top management, motivating managers, compensating managers, and educating and developing managers (Tables 18 and 19, Question 13).

- Budgets should be used to motivate subordinates to increase output and to improve efficiency through participation in managerial planning and control (Table 20, Question 14).

- There can be significant variations across firms in the same industry, either in the proportion of company's higher-level corporate managers with an accounting/finance background or in the size of the corporate budgeting department (Table 21, Question 15).

- Formal budget meetings between corporate and lower-level managers are important and should preferably be conducted once each month (Table 22, Question 16).

- It is useful to subdivide an organization into profit centers, both for domestic and overseas operations, in order to improve performance (Table 23, Question 17).

- Variations in budget policies and procedures across profit centers are desirable (Table 24, Question 18).

- It is preferable to have a fiscal person at the profit center level to coordinate budgetary activities (Table 25, Question 19).

- Profit centers should be encouraged to use computers for budget-related purposes. Their computers should be compatible with corporate computers. Profit center managers should have direct access to their data base (Table 26, Question 20).

- It is preferable to use as many organizational devices as possible to manage corporate–profit center relationships. Annual budgets, capital budgets, informal contacts between corporate and profit center managers, and performance evaluation systems should be emphasized (Tables 27 and 28, Question 21).

These assumptions of corporate top management influence the design as well as the use of budgetary controls. The next chapter describes the features of the long-range planning systems used by the respondents.

4

Long-Range Planning Practices

Ideally, a firm should start its planning process by stating its mission and its objectives. The firm should then formulate a strategy to achieve its long-term objectives. The strategy implementation process requires designing an appropriate organization structure, staffing the organization with qualified people, and developing a suitable planning and control system. The clearer the long-range plan, the clearer the short-run targets. Long-range planning is therefore an important process used by senior managers to translate organizational objectives into an integrated action plan for managers at various levels. The long-range plan, in turn, is used as the basis for preparing annual budgets. This chapter describes selected characteristics of the long-range planning processes used by the respondents, as well as some of the linkages used in translating long-term plans to budgets.

FORMAL PLAN OR BUDGET PERIOD

The plan period used by most firms is either one year or less, or four to five years (Question 22). The two popular time horizons for planning are one year and five years, respectively.

Nearly 55% of the participants report that their planning period is three years or less. The short-term orientation is particularly visible in commercial banks and hospitals where over 50% of the firms have a budget period of one year or less for profits and sales. A plan period of over five years for sales or profits is used by less than 10% of the firms. A notable exception is the utility industry, where the proportion of firms preparing plans for five years or more for sales and profits is 46% and 32%, respectively. Formal long-term planning is therefore not emphasized by most firms, and the primary emphasis is on short- and medium-term planning for sales and profits.

The plan period for expenses is one year or less in 40% of the firms included in the study. Nearly 60% of the firms have a plan period of less than three years for expenses. Once again, the utility industry is the only exception.

Nearly one-fourth of the respondents do not use production targets. The remaining firms, especially those in commercial banking, hospitals, and manufacturing, emphasize a plan period of one year or less for production targets, while a plan period of four years or more is adopted by most utilities, diversified financial, and large manufacturing firms.

Approximately 60% of the participants use a plan period of three years or less for capital expenditures. The proportion of firms using a plan horizon of five years or more for capital expenditures is rather low in commercial banks, diversified financial firms, hospitals, and life insurance companies and quite high in utilities, transportation, and manufacturing.

Market share goals are not established by 31% of the respondents. Regulated industries, such as hospitals, life insurance, and utilities, either do not specify market share targets or use a one-year budget period. Only one-third of the participants established market share targets for four years or more.

Return-on-capital targets are not used by 18% of the participants. Less than one-third of the hospitals and life insurance companies specify a return-on-capital target for one year or more. However, the practice of establishing long-term targets for return on capital for four years or more, is popular in diversified financial firms (50%), large manufacturing companies (49%), and utilities (82%).

Budgets for number of employees are not used by 14% of the respondents. A budget period of one year or less is chosen by 44% of the firms. The one-year budget period was particularly popular among commercial banks and hospitals. Although long-term targets for four or more years for number of employees are used by 30% of the firms, there is considerable variation across the industries, from 5% in hospitals to 48% in utilities.

Commercial banks and hospitals seem to be lagging behind other industries in establishing long-range targets for most areas included in the planning process. Targets for production, market share, return on capital, and number of employees are not established by 14% to 31% of the participants. However, targets for profits, sales, operating expenses, and capital expenditure are used by nearly all participants. Approximately 50% of the participants do not establish any targets beyond three years, while a plan period of over five years is used by less than 10% of the participants. These results suggest that the short- and medium-term targets are stressed during the goal-setting process, and targets beyond five years are rarely used.

FREQUENCY OF UPDATING LONG-RANGE PLANS

Annual updating of long-range plans is the most popular choice in all industries and is used by 85% of the participants (Question 23). Because nearly half the participants use a plan period of three years or less, and annual updating is the most popular choice, it is likely that in many companies, the long-range plan is a mere extrapolation of the annual budget.

MONTHS OF COMMENCEMENT AND COMPLETION OF THE LONG-RANGE PLANNING PROCESS

The long-range planning process usually starts 2 to 18 months before the end of the fiscal year, with nearly half the firms initiating the planning process five to seven months before the end of the fiscal year (Question 23). Most (95%) of the participants complete their long-term plans seven months or less before the end of the fiscal year. Approximately 65% of the firms complete their plans three months or less before the end of the fiscal period. A majority of the firms take five months or less to complete their long-range plans.

TITLE OF THE PERSON PRIMARILY RESPONSIBLE FOR DEVELOPING LONG-RANGE PLAN FOR THE COMPANY

In nearly half the firms, the title of the person responsible for preparing long-range plans is vice president of planning or director of budgets (Question 23; Exhibit I in Appendix I). Senior corporate managers, such as chairman, president, executive vice president, or chief financial officer are responsible for long-term planning in 36% of the firms. These findings suggest that corporate managers consider long-range planning to be an important process.

LINKAGES BETWEEN LONG-RANGE PLANS AND ANNUAL BUDGETS

The numbers used in the first year of the long-range plan and the corresponding year's budget are either identical or almost the same in 62% of the participating firms (Table 29, Question 24). The linkages are quite tight in all industries except commercial banking, diversified finance, and hospitals.

The respondents report an even stronger linkage in the proportion of managers participating in the preparation of both the long-range plan and the operational budget. Thus, a major method used by firms to achieve a strong linkage between long-range plans and operating budgets is to ask some managers involved in long-range planning to also participate in preparing operating budgets (Table 30, Question 24).

A third method of establishing linkages between long- and short-term plans is to break the long-term plans into medium- or short-term projects. This approach to creating the linkages is used by 57% of the participants. More than half of the respondents in each of the industries except transportation use this approach (Table 31, Question 25). Nearly two-thirds of the firms using this approach strengthen their linkages by requiring approval of medium- and short-term projects prior to the commencement of the budget cycle.

Managers consider tight linkages between long-term and medium-term plans to be desirable. Given that nearly 50% of the participants do not establish goals beyond three years, the observed practice of creating tight linkages between the long- and the short-term plans could result in an unintended overemphasis on the short term. Tight linkages could also encourage managers to prepare long-term plans by extrapolating annual goals.

PROPORTION OF PROFIT CENTERS PREPARING LONG-RANGE PLANS

More than three-fourths of the participants prepare long-range plans at their profit center level (Table 32, Question 26). All industries except commercial banks, hospitals, and retailers reported that most or all their profit centers prepared long-term plans.

CONCLUSIONS

About three-fourths of the participants have a fairly sophisticated long-range planning system. Most firms prepare long-range targets in several areas and update them annually. Long-range plans are usually prepared over a period of up to five months. Long-range plans are prepared at the profit center level in nearly three-fourths of all firms. Finally, senior corporate managers are actively involved in preparing long-range plans in about one-third of the firms.

Senior managers therefore seem to consider long-term planning to be an important activity and are willing to invest considerable resources in preparing and using long-term plans. Despite such good intentions, there seems to be an unintended bias in favor of short-term planning because of the emphasis placed on using short- and medium-term planning time horizons, the preferred practice of establishing tight linkages between the long- and short-term plans, and the annual review of long-term

Table 29
Tightness of the Linkage between the Numbers Used in the First Year of the Long-Range Plan and the Corresponding Year's Budget (Question 24)

Tightness of Linkage	Commercial Banks	Diversified Financial	Diversified Service	Hospitals	Life Insurance	Large Manufacturing	Medium Manufacturing	Retailers/ Wholesalers	Transportation	Utilities	Miscellaneous	Total
Identical	9 (26)	2 (17)	9 (41)	4 (17)	12 (55)	37 (36)	16 (44)	9 (43)	5 (46)	14 (50)	6 (35)	123 (38)
Almost the same	9 (26)	5 (42)	8 (36)	5 (22)	4 (18)	18 (18)	10 (28)	5 (24)	2 (18)	8 (28)	4 (24)	78 (24)
Slightly different	13 (37)	4 (33)	3 (14)	12 (52)	5 (23)	40 (40)	6 (17)	7 (33)	3 (27)	5 (18)	5 (29)	103 (31)
Very Different	4 (11)	1 (8)	2 (9)	2 (9)	1 (4)	6 (6)	4 (11)	0 (0)	1 (9)	1 (4)	2 (12)	24 (7)
Total	35 (100)	12 (100)	22 (100)	23 (100)	22 (100)	101 (100)	36 (100)	21 (100)	11 (100)	28 (100)	17 (100)	328 (100)

The entries in each cell are "number of respondents" and ("column percentage") respectively.

Table 30
Proportion of Managers Participating in the Preparation of Long-Range Plans Who Are Also Involved in Developing Budgets (Question 24)

Proportion of Managers	Commercial Banks	Diversified Financial	Diversified Service	Hospitals	Life Insurance	Large Manufacturing	Medium Manufacturing	Retailers/ Wholesalers	Transportation	Utilities	Miscellaneous	Total
No Basis for an opinion	0 (0)	1 (8)	0 (0)	0 (0)	0 (0)	0 (0)	0 (0)	0 (0)	0 (0)	2 (7)	0 (0)	3 (1)
None	0 (0)	0 (0)	1 (4)	1 (4)	0 (0)	2 (2)	1 (3)	1 (5)	0 (0)	0 (0)	0 (0)	6 (2)
Some	12 (33)	3 (23)	5 (23)	12 (50)	5 (23)	12 (12)	8 (21)	7 (33)	5 (42)	9 (32)	4 (24)	82 (25)
Many	10 (28)	2 (15)	3 (14)	3 (13)	3 (14)	15 (15)	4 (11)	5 (24)	2 (16)	5 (18)	5 (29)	57 (17)
Most	14 (39)	7 (54)	13 (59)	8 (33)	14 (63)	71 (71)	24 (65)	8 (38)	5 (42)	12 (43)	8 (47)	184 (55)
Total	36 (100)	13 (100)	22 (100)	24 (100)	22 (100)	100 (100)	37 (100)	21 (100)	12 (100)	28 (100)	17 (100)	332 (100)

The entries in each cell are "number of respondents" and ("column percentage") respectively.

Table 31

Proportion of Companies in which Long-Term Plans Are Broken into Medium- or Short-Term Projects (Question 25)

Are long term plans broken up?	Commercial Banks	Diversified Financial	Diversified Service	Hospitals	Life Insurance	Large Manufacturing	Medium Manufacturing	Retailers/ Wholesalers	Transportation	Utilities	Miscellaneous	Total
No	14 (39)	6 (46)	8 (36)	7 (30)	7 (32)	45 (46)	17 (46)	9 (43)	7 (64)	11 (39)	10 (59)	141 (43)
Yes	22 (61)	7 (54)	14 (64)	16 (70)	15 (68)	53 (54)	20 (54)	12 (57)	4 (36)	17 (61)	7 (41)	187 (57)
Total	36 (100)	13 (100)	22 (100)	23 (100)	22 (100)	98 (100)	37 (100)	21 (100)	11 (100)	28 (100)	17 (100)	328 (100)

The entries in each cell are "number of respondents" and ("column percentage") respectively.

Table 32
Proportion of Profit Centers Preparing Long-Range Plans (Question 26)

Proportion	Commercial Banks	Diversified Financial	Diversified Service	Hospitals	Life Insurance	Large Manu-facturing	Medium Manu-facturing	Retailers/Wholesalers	Transportation	Utilities	Miscellaneous	Total
None	5 (15)	1 (10)	0 (0)	2 (25)	3 (17)	1 (1)	3 (9)	8 (40)	1 (11)	1 (6)	0 (0)	25 (9)
Some	15 (46)	1 (10)	3 (14)	1 (13)	1 (5)	4 (4)	2 (6)	4 (20)	1 (11)	2 (13)	0 (0)	34 (12)
Many	2 (6)	0 (0)	0 (0)	1 (12)	1 (5)	1 (1)	0 (0)	0 (0)	0 (0)	0 (0)	1 (7)	6 (2)
Most	5 (15)	4 (40)	4 (19)	0 (0)	3 (17)	15 (16)	6 (17)	1 (5)	0 (0)	1 (6)	5 (36)	44 (16)
All	6 (18)	4 (40)	14 (67)	4 (50)	10 (56)	74 (78)	24 (68)	7 (35)	7 (78)	12 (75)	8 (57)	170 (61)
Total	33 (100)	10 (100)	21 (100)	8 (100)	18 (100)	95 (100)	35 (100)	20 (100)	9 (100)	16 (100)	14 (100)	279 (100)

The entries in each cell are "number of respondents" and ("column percentage") respectively.

plan targets. Consequently, it is likely that in many companies the long-term plans are mere extrapolations of the annual budget.

The relative emphasis given to long-range planning varies across industries. Commercial banks and hospitals use long-range planning to a lesser extent than other industries. Most firms in utility, manufacturing, diversified service, and transportation industries use a plan period of four years or more. Industries lagging behind in long-range planning practices could benefit by selective adoption of the techniques used by other industries and by offering training programs to develop specific skills in long-range planning. Senior managers should improve the systems used to monitor the long-range planning process so that the long-term plans could be prepared and implemented effectively.

5

Budgetary Practices in the United States

The first chapter pointed out that the earlier comprehensive study of budgetary practices dates back to 1958. The purpose of this chapter is to describe current budgetary practices in the United States. Significant interindustry differences in budgetary practices are also identified and discussed. The final section of the chapter presents a discussion of whether the self-ratings of budgetary effectiveness provided by the respondents are backed by the data on budgetary practices.

The findings are grouped into five broad categories of budgetary practices: forecasting, budgetary policies and procedures, budgetary standards, performance reports, and results. The data are presented by industry. Analysis and implications for managers are discussed for each category of budget practice.

FORECASTING

Preparation of a sales forecast is usually the starting point in the budgetary process. The use of a reasonable forecast that is acceptable to the responsible manager is a prerequisite for effective budgeting. The principal procedures used in preparing various types of forecasts for long-range planning and budgeting are discussed in this section.

Types of Forecasts Used

The participants were asked to specify the frequency with which their firms developed forecasts of general economic conditions, sales estimates for industry, company's market share, and sales estimates for the firm.

Approximately 18% of the firms do not prepare a forecast of the general economic conditions. Over 60% of the firms prepare this forecast annually. Semi-annual and quarterly forecasts are prepared respectively by 4% and 17% of the firms. Over 40% of the hospitals and retailers do not prepare this forecast.

Industry sales estimates are not used by 36% of the participants. Over half the hospitals, retailers, and utilities do not prepare industry sales estimates. These forecasts are prepared annually by nearly 50% of the participants. Nearly two-thirds of the diversified financial and manufacturing firms prepare an annual forecast of industry sales estimates.

Market share forecasts are the least popular and are not used by 40% of the respondents. Diversified financial and manufacturing firms emphasize this forecast, while most service industries do not prepare market share forecasts.

Sales estimates for the company are the most popular type of forecast and are used by 90% of the participants (Table 33, Question 27). Nearly 60% of the respondents prepare their company sales forecasts annually. Quarterly forecasts are used by slightly over 25% of the firms.

The data suggest that many firms prepare only company sales forecasts, while others prepare two or more forecasts. Diversified financial and manufacturing firms frequently use more than one method of forecasting, and they seem to have a systematic approach to preparing budgetary forecasts.

Principal Procedures Used in Preparing Forecasts

Analysis of historical data, closely followed by opinions of company managers, are the most popular approaches to preparing forecasts for both long-range planning and budgeting (Tables 34 and 35, Question 28).

Three-fourths of the participants frequently use analysis of historical data to prepare long-range plans, and only 5% state that they never use this approach. A significantly higher proportion of firms in nonfinancial service industries use this technique frequently. Opinions of company managers are almost as popular as analysis of historical data. Manufacturing and diversified services firms are the most frequent users of company managers' opinions. Industry analysis is used frequently by slightly over 50% of the participants, more so by the manufacturing firms. It is surprising to note that 40% of the retailers never use industry analysis in their long-range planning. Outside consultants are rarely used for long-range planning, especially by retail firms. Economic models are used by over 60% of the respondents for long-range planning. A greater proportion of utilities and transportation firms use economic models for long-range planning.

Almost all firms use both analysis of historical data and opinions of company managers in preparing sales forecasts for use in budgeting. Manufacturing firms rely more heavily on opinions of company managers, while hospitals and retailers place a greater emphasis on analysis of historical data. Industry analysis is used in preparing sales forecasts for budgets in about 85% of the firms. Manufacturing firms use industry analysis very frequently, but 40% of the retailers do not use this technique. Outside consultants are rarely used in preparing sales forecasts, especially in diversified financial and retail firms. Nearly 60% of the participating firms use economic models to prepare their budgetary sales forecasts. Over 80% of the retailers do not use economic models, and nearly 70% of utilities use the approach extensively.

Although the respondents use historical data quite frequently, they also emphasize opinions of company managers in preparing sales forecasts for both long-range planning and budgeting. Economic models are emphasized by 9% of the participants in long-range planning, but the proportion comes down to 3% for budgeting.

In general, the respondents prepare sales forecasts both for long-range planning and for budgeting by relying on internal

Table 33
Period Covered by Forecast of Company Sales (Question 27)

Period covered by forecast	Commercial Banks	Diversified Financial	Diversified Service	Hospitals	Life Insurance	Large Manufacturing	Medium Manufacturing	Retailers/ Wholesalers	Transportation	Utilities	Miscellaneous	Total
Not covered	14 (30)	0 (0)	4 (18)	2 (5)	2 (8)	10 (10)	0 (0)	1 (4)	4 (24)	0 (0)	0 (0)	37 (10)
Quarterly	11 (23)	3 (21)	5 (23)	4 (11)	4 (16)	37 (37)	13 (32)	11 (39)	4 (23)	5 (19)	7 (35)	104 (27)
Semi-Annual	2 (4)	0 (0)	0 (0)	2 (5)	0 (0)	3 (3)	0 (0)	4 (14)	2 (12)	3 (12)	0 (0)	16 (4)
Annual	20 (43)	11 (79)	13 (59)	30 (79)	19 (76)	51 (50)	28 (68)	12 (43)	7 (41)	18 (69)	13 (65)	222 (59)
Total	47 (100)	14 (100)	22 (100)	38 (100)	25 (100)	101 (100)	41 (100)	28 (100)	17 (100)	26 (100)	20 (100)	379 (100)

The entries in each cell are "number of respondents" and ("column percentage") respectively.

Table 34
Procedures Used in Sales Forecasting for Long-Range Planning (Question 28) (Percentages)

	Commercial Banks	Diversified Financial	Diversified Service	Hospitals	Life Insurance	Large Manu-facturing	Medium Manu-facturing	Retailers/ Wholesalers	Transporta-tion	Utilities	Miscella-neous	Total
Analysis of Historical Data												
– Not Used	12	8	0	11	5	2	0	8	8	4	0	5
– Used Occasionally	17	17	21	25	16	24	35	0	8	8	27	20
– Used Frequently	71	75	79	64	79	74	65	92	84	88	73	75
Opinion of Company Mgrs.												
– Not Used	12	9	0	14	0	1	0	12	31	4	7	6
– Use Occasionally	26	27	16	43	21	13	11	24	8	20	20	20
– Used Frequently	62	64	84	43	79	86	89	64	61	76	73	74
Industry Analysis												
– Not Used	23	10	10	26	20	4	9	40	8	24	19	15
– Used Occasionally	33	40	57	41	50	26	23	40	33	28	37	34
– Used Frequently	44	50	33	33	30	70	68	20	59	48	44	51
Outside Consultants												
– Not used	64	38	76	42	55	58	78	92	54	52	60	61
– Used Occasionally	28	39	24	48	45	36	16	8	31	44	33	32
– Used Frequently	8	23	0	10	0	6	6	0	15	4	7	7
Economic Models												
– Not Used	43	42	38	41	45	31	55	71	15	4	43	38
– Used Occasionally	26	33	57	48	40	44	24	21	62	24	29	37
– Used Frequently	31	25	5	11	15	25	21	8	23	72	28	25

Table 35
Procedures Used in Sales Forecasting for Budgeting (Question 28) (Percentages)

	Commercial Banks	Diversified Financial	Diversified Service	Hospitals	Life Insurance	Large Manufacturing	Medium Manufacturing	Retailers/ Wholesalers	Transportation	Utilities	Miscellaneous	Total
Analysis of Historical Data												
– Not Used	0	0	0	0	0	2	3	0	0	0	5	1
– Used Occasionally	13	7	15	8	12	23	22	0	12	7	10	14
– Used Frequently	87	93	85	92	88	75	75	100	88	93	85	85
Opinions of Company Mgrs.												
– Not Used	2	0	0	3	0	1	0	0	12	4	0	2
– Used Occasionally	13	8	10	44	12	10	3	22	0	19	15	14
– Used Frequently	85	92	90	53	88	89	97	78	88	77	85	84
Industry Analysis												
– Not Used	20	17	16	21	21	5	10	40	12	23	21	16
– Used Occasionally	47	42	32	53	58	25	30	36	44	35	42	37
– Used Frequently	33	41	52	26	21	70	60	24	44	42	37	47
Outside Consultants												
– Not Used	75	91	80	59	79	70	87	96	59	62	81	74
– Used Occasionally	16	9	20	30	21	24	8	4	29	27	19	20
– Used Frequently	9	0	0	11	0	6	5	0	12	11	0	6
Economic Models												
– Not Used	38	50	37	40	59	35	62	83	35	4	53	43
– Used Occasionally	29	42	58	38	32	45	20	13	30	29	29	34
– Used Frequently	33	8	5	22	9	20	18	4	35	67	18	23

sources of information such as analysis of historical data or opinions of company managers. Industry analysis and economic models are not being used as frequently as one would expect, especially in a dynamic industry such as retailing. Outside consultants are seldom used. Apparently, the industry is relying heavily on internally generated data. Managers may want to examine whether increased use of industry data and economic models could enhance the accuracy of their sales forecasts.

BUDGETARY POLICIES AND PROCEDURES

The responses to the questions on budgetary policies and procedures are presented and discussed in this section.

Scheduling and Monitoring Budget Preparation

Major activities or projects are frequently monitored by using Gantt charts, the Critical Path Method (CPM), and the Program Evaluation and Review Technique (PERT). The responses (Table 36, Question 29) show that each of these techniques is used by less than one-fourth of the respondents. CPM is relatively more popular. Diversified services, hospitals, retailers, and medium manufacturing firms use these techniques less frequently. Although budgeting is rated as the most important organizational device for managing corporate–profit center relationships, and because managers invest substantial amounts of their time in preparing budgets, managers do not use scientific techniques to schedule and monitor the preparation of budgets.

Commencement and Completion of Budgeting

Most firms commence their budgetary process four to six months before the end of the fiscal period and complete it in the last two months of the fiscal year (Question 29). The budgetary process usually takes about four months in most firms.

The Fiscal Period

Nearly two-thirds of the respondents state that their fiscal year begins in January (Question 29). Nearly 80% of the hospitals and about 13% of the participants start their fiscal period in October.

Table 36
Techniques Used for Scheduling and Monitoring the Preparation of Budgets (Question 29)

Percentage of Respondents Using the Technique in

Technique Used	Commercial Banks	Diversified Financial	Diversified Service	Hospitals	Life Insurance	Large Manufacturing	Medium Manufacturing	Retailers/ Wholesalers	Transportation	Utilities	Miscellaneous	Total
1.Gantt Charts	24	33	10	16	9	12	6	11	15	12	10	13
2.Critical Path Method (CPM)	24	31	10	16	17	22	16	11	27	44	25	22
3.Program evaluation and Review Technique (PERT)	17	23	5	13	22	20	17	15	29	12	30	18

Specific Budgetary Practices

Budget manuals are used by nearly two-thirds of the firms (Table 37, Question 30). Medium manufacturing, retailing, and transportation industries use budget manuals less frequently. Over 90% of the diversified financial firms use budget manuals.

Nearly 90% of the respondents use preprinted budget forms. Almost all firms in commercial banking and diversified financial industries, but only 76% of the transportation firms, use preprinted forms.

Nearly 40% of the participants use a formal procedure for evaluating the extent to which budgets are prepared and used effectively (see Exhibit II in Appendix I). A much higher proportion (60%) of the diversified financial firms use such a formal procedure. However, over 70% of diversified service, large manufacturing, and transportation firms do not use formal procedures for evaluating budgetary effectiveness.

Diversified financial firms have adopted formal budgetary practices more readily than other industries, especially transportation. Although several approaches used in budgeting were originally developed in the manufacturing sector, the data suggest that manufacturing firms are using some procedures less frequently than other industries.

Comprehensive Budgetary Procedures

Nearly two-thirds of the participating firms use detailed and comprehensive procedures for over 60% of the budgeting activities (Table 38, Question 31). Diversified financial, life insurance, and utilities industries emphasize formal procedures in budgetary activities, while diversified services, medium manufacturing, retailing, and transportation sectors use fewer formal procedures. Smaller firms, such as those in medium manufacturing, probably do not need formal procedures.

Significant Change in Budgetary Policies

Nearly 60% of the respondents state that they made a significant change in their budgetary processes during the past

Table 37
Percentage of Firms Using Specific Budgetary Practices (Question 30)

Budgeting Practice	Commercial Banks	Diversified Financial	Diversified Service	Hospitals	Life Insurance	Large Manu- facturing	Medium Manu- facturing	Retailers/ Wholesalers	Transporta- tion	Utilities	Miscella- neous	Total
Use of a budget manual	69	93	55	61	72	71	49	46	53	66	67	64
Use of preprinted budget forms	98	100	86	90	96	87	88	86	76	89	80	89
Use of a formal procedure for evaluating the extent to which budgets are prepared and used effectively by management	50	60	18	54	48	28	32	36	18	33	58	38

All numbers are percentages unless otherwise stated; add vertically to 100%.

Table 38
Relative Proportion of Budgetary Activities for which Detailed Comprehensive Procedures Are Used (Question 31)

Relative Proportion	Comercial Banks	Diversified Financial	Diversified Service	Hospitals	Life Insurance	Large Manufacturing	Medium Manufacturing	Retailers/ Wholesalers	Transportation	Utilities	Miscellaneous	Total
0%	0 (0)	0 (0)	0 (0)	0 (0)	0 (0)	0 (0)	0 (0)	2 (7)	0 (0)	0 (0)	1 (5)	3 (1)
20%	1 (2)	2 (13)	3 (15)	4 (11)	1 (4)	14 (13)	4 (10)	7 (25)	2 (12)	2 (7)	0 (0)	40 (11)
40%	7 (16)	1 (7)	8 (40)	9 (25)	6 (26)	22 (21)	11 (28)	3 (11)	7 (41)	3 (11)	4 (21)	81 (21)
60%	18 (40)	2 (13)	4 (20)	6 (16)	4 (18)	34 (32)	12 (30)	7 (25)	4 (23)	8 (30)	9 (47)	108 (29)
80%	15 (33)	9 (60)	5 (25)	15 (42)	9 (39)	30 (29)	12 (30)	6 (21)	3 (18)	10 (37)	3 (16)	117 (31)
100%	4 (9)	1 (7)	0 (0)	2 (6)	3 (13)	5 (5)	1 (2)	3 (11)	1 (6)	4 (15)	2 (11)	26 (7)
Total	45 (100)	15 (100)	20 (100)	36 (100)	23 (100)	105 (100)	40 (100)	28 (100)	17 (100)	27 (100)	19 (100)	375 (100)

The entries in each cell are "number of respondents" and ("column percentage") respectively.

77

three years (Table 39, Question 40). Over one-third of the commercial banks, diversified financial firms, and hospitals report that they made significant changes in their budgetary practices during the past year. Thus, substantial changes have been made in budgeting during the past three years. Given the long history of budgeting, changes in a large cross section of the industry are surprising.

BUDGETARY STANDARDS

A major purpose of budgeting is to provide a standard or yard-stick to measure, control, or evaluate current performance. This section reports budgetary practices in establishing these standards.

Standards for Sales or Service Revenues

Sales budgets are used by nearly three-fourths of the companies to specify revenue targets (Table 40, Question 33). Use of historical data and sales forecasts hold the second and third ranks, respectively, based on the frequency of usage. Diversified financial firms and utilities do not use these items as standards for sales/service revenues. Nearly 70% of the firms use two or three sources to specify their revenue standards.

Standards for Costs and Expenses

Use of historical costs (80%) and budgets for overhead expenses (73%) are the popular sources for establishing standards for costs and expenses (Table 41, Question 34). Over 50% of the respondents state that they use six or more sources of information for establishing standards for costs and expenses. The data suggest that the participants place a heavy emphasis on standard setting and that the use of multiple sources of information for establishing standards is a common practice.

Communication of Responsibilities to Managers

Formal conferences (72%) and copies of the operating plan are the major means of communicating the responsibilities to senior

Table 39
Date on which the Last Significant Change Was Made in the Budgetary Policies, Procedures, or Practices (Question 40)

Date on Which Change was made	Commercial Banks	Diversified Financial	Diversified Service	Hospitals	Life Insurance	Large Manu-facturing	Medium Manu-facturing	Retailers/ Wholesalers	Transporta-tion	Utilities	Miscella-neous	Total
Less than one year ago	17 (36)	6 (40)	4 (18)	14 (35)	7 (28)	29 (27)	9 (22)	4 (14)	5 (30)	6 (23)	4 (21)	105 (27)
1 to 3 years ago	16 (33)	5 (33)	6 (27)	14 (35)	9 (36)	27 (26)	18 (44)	6 (22)	6 (35)	4 (15)	6 (32)	117 (30)
More than three years ago	15 (31)	4 (27)	12 (55)	12 (30)	9 (36)	50 (47)	14 (34)	18 (64)	6 (35)	16 (62)	9 (47)	165 (43)
Total	48 (100)	15 (100)	22 (100)	40 (100)	25 (100)	106 (100)	41 (100)	28 (100)	17 (100)	26 (100)	19 (100)	387 (100)

The entries in each cell are "number of respondents" and ("column percentage") respectively.

Table 40
Percentage of Firms Using Specific Standards to Measure, Control, and/or Evaluate Sales/Service Revenues (Question 33)

Standard Used	Commercial Banks	Diversified Financial	Diversified Service	Hospitals	Life Insurance	Large Manufacturing	Medium Manufacturing	Retailers/ Wholesalers	Transportation	Utilities	Miscellaneous	Total
1. Historical Revenue Data	80	53	73	78	68	74	63	79	76	41	75	71
2. Sales Forecasts	41	53	50	41	84	79	98	54	59	52	75	65
3. Sales Budgets	78	67	77	51	60	85	85	68	65	50	90	74
4. Sales Quotes	8	33	14	0	24	29	37	11	24	4	45	21

Table 41
Percentage of Firms Using Specific Standards to Measure, Control, and/or Evaluate Actual Costs and Expenses (Question 34)

Standard Used	Commercial Banks	Diversified Financial	Diversified Service	Hospitals	Life Insurance	Large Manufacturing	Medium Manufacturing	Retailers/ Wholesalers	Transportation	Utilities	Miscellaneous	Total
1. Use of Historical Costs	82	80	82	88	96	80	68	79	88	74	76	80
2. Labor Standards	14	7	36	49	8	72	71	54	35	19	52	46
3. Materials Standards	2	0	18	15	0	71	61	18	29	15	43	35
4. Standard Costs	27	13	18	10	32	81	68	21	24	22	48	44
5. Cost Ratios	43	67	48	22	76	60	61	39	53	30	43	50
6. Direct/Variable Costs	20	27	36	24	20	65	59	36	41	15	43	41
7. Budgets for Materials /Expense Cost	29	13	45	71	0	72	44	21	35	78	57	50
8. Budgets for overhead Expense/Cost	43	33	55	37	24	83	66	46	53	59	67	58
9. Budgets for Labor	47	60	64	78	32	77	54	46	47	78	67	63
10. Budgets for Selling Expenses	53	47	68	7	72	87	95	71	41	33	81	65
11. Budgets for Overhead Expenses	78	67	73	22	80	91	95	79	53	41	76	73

managers (Table 42, Question 35). Informal conferences (57%) and the operating plan (51%) are emphasized at the middle management level, and informal conferences (42%) are the major communication channel at the supervisor/foreman level. Thus, the top management emphasizes formal processes in communicating responsibilities to senior managers, while informal conferences provide the major communication channel between middle and lower-level managers.

Time Period Covered by Budgets

Budgets are prepared annually and are broken down either by quarters (79%) or by months (11%) in most firms (Table 43, Question 36). Quarterly budgetary targets are therefore available in about 90% of the firms.

Techniques/Approaches Used in Preparing Budgets

Although most managerial accounting texts strongly advocate the use of flexible budgets, it is rather surprising to note that only 27% of the respondents use flexible budgeting (Table 44, Questions 34, 36, 37, and 38). Manufacturing and diversified financial firms use flexible budgeting more frequently.

Expenses are classified into controllable and noncontrollable categories in 54% of the firms. Contingency plans/budgets and rolling budgets are used in 34% and 21% of the participating firms, respectively. Budgets are subdivided by product lines in about 60% of the firms. It is worth noting that although these basic techniques are quite easy to implement and their usefulness beyond doubt, many participants do not use them. Despite significant changes introduced in budgeting in over 60% of the firms during the past three years, these simple techniques have not been adopted by many firms. However, in over 90% of the firms, budgets are subdivided by major organizational subunits.

Level of Sophistication of Budgetary Procedures

The major conclusion that emerges from the previous analysis is that there is adequate scope for improving the level of sophisti-

Table 42
Percentage of Respondents Using Specific Practices to Communicate Responsibilities to Managers (Question 35)

Practice Used	Commercial Banks	Diversified Financial	Diversified Service	Hospitals	Life Insurance	Large Manufacturing	Medium Manufacturing	Retailers/ Wholesalers	Transportation	Utilities	Miscellaneous	Total
1. Use of Formal Conferences for Senior Managers	90	67	77	66	64	76	80	61	59	62	60	72
2. Use of Formal Conferences for Middle Management	31	33	36	41	24	37	39	29	24	35	40	35
3. Use of Formal Conferences for Supervisors/Foremen	14	20	23	22	4	11	15	4	12	8	10	13
4. Use of Informal Conferences for Senior Managers	24	27	50	37	28	36	29	32	24	31	35	33
5. Use of Informal Conferences for Middle Management	59	60	73	63	64	58	46	61	29	38	70	57
6. Use of Informal Conferences for Supervisors/Foremen	41	53	36	37	40	44	49	43	24	38	50	42
7. Use of Copy of Operating Plan for Senior Managers	53	93	68	73	64	64	71	61	53	46	70	64
8. Use of Copy of Operating Plan for Middle Management	53	47	50	46	60	49	46	54	65	50	50	51
9. Use of Copy of Operating Plan for Supervisors/Foremen	37	13	23	17	16	21	12	18	6	12	20	20

Table 43
Time Period Covered by Budget (Question 36)

Time period Covered	Commercial Banks	Diversified Financial	Diversified Service	Hospitals	Life Insurance	Large Manu-facturing	Medium Manu-facturing	Retailers/ Wholesalers	Transporta-tion	Utilities	Miscella-neous	Total
Multi-year broken up by years or quarters	0 (0)	1 (7)	0 (0)	0 (0)	2 (8)	5 (4)	2 (5)	1 (4)	0 (0)	3 (11)	0 (0)	14 (3)
Annually, broken down by months	6 (13)	2 (13)	2 (9)	2 (5)	11 (44)	11 (10)	4 (10)	3 (11)	1 (6)	1 (4)	1 (5)	44 (11)
Annually, broken down by quarters	41 (85)	12 (80)	20 (91)	39 (95)	11 (44)	85 (79)	32 (78)	16 (57)	15 (88)	21 (78)	17 (81)	309 (79)
Quarterly, broken down by months	1 (2)	0 (0)	0 (0)	0 (0)	0 (0)	1 (1)	0 (0)	7 (25)	1 (6)	0 (0)	1 (5)	11 (3)
Semi-annually, broken down by months	0 (0)	0 (0)	0 (0)	0 (0)	0 (0)	3 (3)	1 (2)	0 (0)	0 (0)	0 (0)	0 (0)	4 (1)
Other	0 (0)	0 (0)	0 (0)	0 (0)	1 (4)	3 (3)	2 (5)	1 (3)	0 (0)	2 (7)	2 (9)	11 (3)
Total	48 (100)	15 (100)	22 (100)	41 (100)	25 (100)	108 (100)	41 (100)	28 (100)	17 (100)	27 (100)	21 (100)	393 (100)

The entries in each cell are "number of respondents" and ("column percentage") respectively.

Table 44
Percentage of Respondents Using Specific Approaches in Preparing Budgets or Performance Reports (Questions 34, 36, 37, 38)

Approach Used	Commercial Banks	Diversified Financial	Diversified Service	Hospitals	Life Insurance	Large Manufacturing	Medium Manufacturing	Retailers/ Wholesalers	Transportation	Utilities	Miscellaneous	Total
1. Use of Flexible budgets in preparing performance reports	13	31	14	27	12	42	39	22	18	15	25	27
2. Classification of expenses into controllable /noncontrollable categories in preparing performance reports	65	53	64	39	56	50	61	64	50	48	48	54
3. Contingency plans/ Budgets	29	20	18	32	28	43	34	36	25	41	25	34
4. Rolling Budgets	18	7	5	14	4	27	33	28	24	17	25	21
5. Subdivide budget by product lines	33	73	77	32	80	71	85	44	41	39	68	60
6. Subdivide budget by major subunits of the company	100	100	95	85	88	93	92	96	88	85	85	92
7. A separate performance Report is Prepared for each department or profit center	98	100	95	95	100	96	95	100	88	100	91	96

cation of budgetary processes by introducing some of the simple techniques just discussed. The data suggest that the level of sophistication of budgetary procedures is lower in the service sector.

PERFORMANCE REPORTS

Performance reports compare actuals with budget standards. Such reports will be useful only if they are matched with the recipient's authority and responsibility, and if they are prepared and reviewed frequently. This section examines whether the performance reports used by the respondents are useful criteria.

Extent to Fit with a Manager's Authority and Responsibility

Over 70% of the respondents reported that "many," "most," or "all" performance reports used by them are matched with each manager's authority and responsibility (Table 45, Question 32). It is quite alarming to note that in nearly 30% of the firms there is an insufficient match between the performance reports and the responsibility structure, since it violates the basic premise of responsibility accounting, of which budgeting is a part.

Performance Reports by Profit Centers

Over 90% of the firms prepare a separate performance report for each department or profit center (Table 44), and this finding is consistent across industries. Although it is encouraging to learn that performance reports are prepared by profit centers, it should be remembered that there is an insufficient fit between performance reports and authority and responsibility structure (Table 45). Unless the performance reports are well matched with the responsibility structure, the budgetary process will be suboptimal. Budgetary targets are frequently broken down by quarters (Table 43); but most firms prepare performance reports each month (Question 38). Ideally, the time periods used in specifying budgetary targets and those in performance reports should match.

Table 45

Proportion of Control Reports which are Matched with a Manager's Organizational Authority and Responsibility (Question 32)

Proportion of control reports	Commercial Banks	Diversified Financial	Diversified Service	Hospitals	Life Insurance	Large Manu-facturing	Medium Manu-facturing	Retailers/ Wholesalers	Transporta-tion	Utilities	Miscella-neous	Total
None	2 (4)	0 (0)	3 (14)	4 (10)	5 (22)	5 (5)	1 (2)	2 (7)	4 (24)	1 (4)	2 (10)	29 (8)
Some	5 (11)	4 (29)	6 (27)	12 (31)	4 (17)	21 (20)	5 (12)	8 (30)	5 (29)	4 (15)	5 (25)	79 (21)
Many	9 (19)	3 (22)	1 (4)	8 (20)	2 (9)	19 (18)	9 (22)	2 (7)	3 (18)	0 (0)	3 (15)	59 (15)
Most	21 (45)	3 (21)	9 (41)	10 (26)	7 (30)	41 (40)	22 (54)	12 (45)	0 (0)	14 (52)	6 (30)	145 (38)
All	10 (21)	4 (28)	3 (14)	5 (13)	5 (22)	18 (17)	4 (10)	3 (11)	5 (29)	8 (29)	4 (20)	69 (18)
Total	47 (100)	14 (100)	22 (100)	39 (100)	23 (100)	104 (100)	41 (100)	27 (100)	17 (100)	27 (100)	20 (100)	381 (100)

The entries in each cell are "number of respondents" and ("column percentage") respectively.

Dealing with Significant Variances

Written explanation of the causes of deviations (67%) and discussion of deviations with immediate superior (56%) are the most popular approaches used in dealing with significant variances (Table 46, Question 39). Written explanations are emphasized in utilities, diversified services, life insurance, and large manufacturing firms, while discussion of the deviations is popular in hospitals. Discussion with immediate superior is also emphasized by commercial banks, medium manufacturing firms, and retailers. Oral discussions are least popular in all industries except hospitals and are used by only 39% of the respondents.

Usefulness of Performance Reports

The previous responses suggest that performance reports are prepared frequently and by department or profit center. However, insufficient fit between performance reports and responsibility structure is probably preventing managers from maximizing the usefulness of performance reports. Similarly, if the time periods used in target setting and performance reporting are matched, performance reports will be easier to understand. Managers should examine whether their firms require any changes in these two areas and take the necessary corrective action.

CONSEQUENCES OF BUDGETING

Companies with effective budgetary control systems are unlikely to face dysfunctional behaviors, and their managers are likely to be satisfied with the effectiveness of their budgetary controls. This section describes the results along these two dimensions.

Budgetary Games

Game playing is reported the least by retailers, transportation firms, and hospitals. Diversified service, diversified finance, utilities, and large manufacturing industries experience high

Table 46
Approach Used in Dealing with a Significant Deviation from the Company's Standards of Performance or Budget (Question 39)

Approach Used	Commercial Banks	Diversified Financial	Diversified Service	Hospitals	Life Insurance	Large Manufacturing	Medium Manufacturing	Retailers/ Wholesalers	Transportation	Utilities	Miscellaneous	Total
1. Written explanation of the Causes of deviation	61	73	82	56	84	76	34	54	65	85	75	67
2. An Indication of Corrective Action taken	37	40	57	35	52	52	30	39	29	52	48	44
3. Discussion of deviation with immediate superior	65	60	55	78	16	50	65	64	47	44	57	56
4. An Oral Discussion	41	33	36	53	36	37	44	39	18	44	24	39

The entries in each cell are "percentage of respondents."

levels of budgetary games. Deferring a needed expenditure is used with the highest frequency, especially in the diversified services industry (Table 47, Question 41). Getting approvals after money was spent, shifting funds between accounts to avoid budget overruns, and employment of contract labor to avoid exceeding headcount limits are the other relatively popular games. Almost all respondents state that they engage in one or more of the budget games. The widespread practice of budget games is a matter of grave concern because it is a symptom of a serious problem. Managers either did not accept the budgetary targets and opted to beat the system, or they felt pressured to achieve the budgetary targets at any cost. Either type of problem is undesirable, and the situation suggests that there is a need to increase the acceptability of budgetary targets in order to obtain the commitment of the managers toward achieving them.

Self-ratings of Budgetary Effectiveness

Nearly 80% of the respondents rate their budgetary effectiveness as either "good" or "extremely effective" (Table 48, Question 42). The reported self-ratings are particularly high in diversified finance, large manufacturing, transportation, and utilities. These performance ratings seem to suggest that the managers are quite satisfied with the quality of their budgetary processes.

Interpretation of Results

The earlier sections of this chapter revealed that most firms could improve their budgetary effectiveness through improved sales forecasting, more realistic standard setting, more frequent use of some proven procedures and techniques, and finally more meaningful performance reports. However, the self-ratings of budgetary effectiveness seem to suggest that the current budgetary practices are quite close to the optimal level and that no major changes are needed. Obviously, there is a contradiction here, and a careful examination of the budgetary practices indicates that the self-ratings of budgetary effectiveness are higher than what they should be. The fact that the managers

Table 47
Frequency with which Different Budget Games Were Played by Managers in Order to Comply with Budgetary Controls (Question 41)

Games playing behavior	Commercial Banks	Diversified Financial	Diversified Service	Hospitals	Life Insurance	Large Manufacturing	Medium Manufacturing	Retailers/ Wholesalers	Transportation	Utilities	Miscellaneous	Total
Employed contract labor to get needed work done, while staying within headcount limits	2.6	2.6	2.3	2.3	2.1	2.5	2.4	2.1	1.7	1.9	2.8	2.6	2.3 (382)
Got required approvals after money was spent in order to speed up the process	2.3	2.3	2.9	2.4	2.3	2.4	2.6	2.0	2.4	2.4	2.4	2.4 (383)
Bought equipment from outside the company, so that the design portion of the expenditure could be capitalized, even though it could have been designed within the company	1.5	1.9	2.0	1.5	1.5	1.7	1.6	1.3	1.5	1.9	1.7	1.6 (367)
Shifted funds between accounts to avoid budget overruns	2.5	2.5	2.5	2.2	2.3	2.4	2.1	1.9	1.9	2.6	2.3	2.3 (383)
Pulled profits from a future period by												
a. deferring a needed expenditure	2.4	2.7	2.9	2.1	2.3	2.7	2.6	2.2	1.9	2.6	2.3	2.5 (381)
b. accelerating a sale	2.1	2.5	2.4	1.1	2.3	2.3	2.5	1.7	1.4	1.5	1.8	2.0 (370)
c. accelerating capital expenditure or expenses because funds were available	2.5	2.4	2.5	2.2	2.3	2.5	2.1	20	1.9	2.7	2.3	2.3 (378)
Total Score for the Industry	15.9	16.9	17.5	13.6	15.5	16.4	15.6	12.8	12.9	16.5	15.4	15.4

The entry in each cell is the weighted average score for the frequency of game playing, on a five-point scale with 1 = never to 5 = almost always. Numbers in parentheses indicate the number of participants who responded to the question.

Table 48
Self-Ratings for Effectiveness of Budgetary Processes Used (Question 42)

Ratings for effectiveness	Commercial Banks	Diversified Financial	Diversified Service	Hospitals	Life Insurance	Large Manu-facturing	Medium Manu-facturing	Retailers/ Wholesalers	Transporta-tion	Utilities	Miscella-neous	Total
Ineffective	0 (0)	0 (0)	0 (0)	0 (0)	0 (0)	0 (0)	0 (0)	0 (0)	1 (6)	0 (0)	1 (5)	2 (1)
Poor	2 (4)	0 (0)	0 (0)	2 (5)	0 (0)	2 (2)	3 (7)	3 (11)	1 (6)	0 (0)	0 (0)	13 (3)
Neither poor nor good	8 (17)	1 (7)	5 (23)	8 (19)	6 (24)	17 (16)	12 (29)	4 (14)	1 (6)	2 (7)	6 (30)	70 (18)
Good	32 (65)	12 (80)	17 (77)	27 (66)	16 (64)	74 (68)	16 (39)	17 (61)	12 (70)	21 (78)	11 (55)	255 (65)
Extremely effective	7 (14)	2 (13)	0 (0)	4 (10)	3 (12)	15 (14)	10 (25)	4 (14)	2 (12)	4 (15)	2 (10)	53 (13)
Total	49 (100)	15 (100)	22 (100)	41 (100)	25 (100)	108 (100)	41 (100)	28 (100)	17 (100)	27 (100)	20 (100)	393 (100)

The entries in each cell are "number of respondents" and ("column percentage") respectively.

rated their performance so high could mean that they believe that no major improvements could be made in budgetary processes. Managers also may have become complacent. To avoid complacency and stagnation, periodic management audits of budgetary processes should be undertaken. Areas of deficiency identified during such audits should be rectified expeditiously.

6

Budget Manager Characteristics

Part V of the questionnaire focused on the person primarily responsible for the financial expression of the combined objectives and goals of various organizational units in the form of coordinated plan of operations or budgets for the top management. This chapter describes the characteristics of the budget manager.

TITLE AND REPORTING RELATIONSHIPS

The budget manager has the title of vice president of planning or director of budgets in 56% of the firms, and vice president–finance or chief financial officer in about 10% of the companies (Question 43; Exhibit I in Appendix I). The corporate controller performs this role in 14% of the firms. These titles suggest that the budget manager occupies a reasonably high corporate position in most firms. The importance accorded to budgeting is indirectly reflected in the influential titles given to budget managers.

Nearly one-third of the budget managers report to the corporate controller. Budget managers report to either the vice president–planning or vice president–finance in 38% of the firms. The budget manager directly reports to the chairman or the president in 14% of the firms. Thus, budget managers generally report to senior corporate managers.

YEAR OF ESTABLISHMENT OF THE BUDGET MANAGER'S POSITION

The budget manager's position was established before 1970 in 27% of the firms (Table 49, Question 43). Nearly 40% of the diversified service and large manufacturing firms had a budget manager before 1970, while less than 15% of the firms in each of the categories of diversified finance, life insurance, and transportation had established the position before 1970.

Nearly 30% of the respondents state that the position was established during 1978-1981. Of the firms in diversified finance, hospitals, medium manufacturing, and transportation, over 40% in each introduced the position during 1978-1981.

Although only 18% of the participants established the budget manager's position after 1981, 38% of the transportation firms and 29% of the diversified finance companies did not have a budget manager until 1981. Budgeting is probably in its infancy in these two service industries.

EDUCATIONAL BACKGROUND

Nearly half the budget managers held graduate degrees (Table 50, Question 43). The most common educational background, found in 30% of budget managers, is a non-MBA graduate degree with professional certification. Graduate degree holders are more likely to be found in those industries where the budget manager's position was established recently (see Exhibit III in Appendix I). The presence of nonaccounting undergraduate degree holders with professional certification is relatively more frequent in manufacturing firms and hospitals. Manufacturing firms have a lower proportion of MBA degree holders than other industries. In general, the educational level of budget managers is lower in manufacturing firms.

Table 49
Year of Establishment of the Budget Manager's Position (Question 43)

Year of Establishment	Commercial Banks	Diversified Financial	Diversified Service	Hospitals	Life Insurance	Large Manufacturing	Medium Manufacturing	Retailers/ Wholesalers	Transportation	Utilities	Miscellaneous	Total
1970 or before	10 (31)	1 (14)	6 (38)	6 (25)	1 (6)	25 (40)	5 (20)	3 (21)	2 (12)	4 (20)	3 (38)	66 (27)
1971 – 77	8 (25)	1 (14)	4 (25)	3 (12)	8 (50)	18 (28)	3 (12)	5 (36)	1 (6)	8 (40)	0 (0)	59 (25)
1978 – 81	7 (22)	3 (43)	4 (25)	10 (42)	6 (38)	10 (16)	11 (44)	5 (36)	7 (44)	6 (30)	4 (50)	73 (30)
1982 +	7 (22)	2 (29)	2 (12)	5 (21)	1 (6)	10 (16)	6 (24)	1 (7)	6 (38)	2 (10)	1 (12)	43 (18)
Total	32 (100)	7 (100)	16 (100)	24 (100)	16 (100)	63 (100)	25 (100)	14 (100)	16 (100)	20 (100)	8 (100)	241 (100)

The entries in each cell are "number of respondents" and ("column percentage") respectively.

Table 50
Educational Background of the Budget Manager (Question 43)

Educational Background of Budget Manager	Commercial Banks	Diversified Financial	Diversified Service	Hospitals	Life Insurance	Large Manufacturing	Medium Manufacturing	Retailers/ Wholesalers	Transportation	Utilities	Miscellaneous	Total
Junior College and Prof. certification	3 (8)	0 (0)	2 (12)	5 (17)	0 (0)	8 (11)	3 (10)	1 (6)	0 (0)	1 (4)	2 (17)	25 (9)
Non-accounting undergraduate	0 (0)	2 (18)	0 (0)	0 (0)	3 (17)	2 (3)	2 (7)	0 (0)	1 (6)	0 (0)	0 (0)	10 (4)
Non-accounting undergraduate with prof. certification	4 (11)	1 (9)	2 (12)	8 (28)	3 (17)	14 (19)	6 (21)	3 (17)	3 (18)	3 (14)	1 (8)	48 (16)
Accounting undergraduate	4 (10)	1 (9)	2 (11)	0 (0)	2 (11)	8 (11)	3 (10)	0 (0)	1 (6)	1 (5)	2 (17)	24 (9)
Accounting undergraduate with prof.certification	9 (24)	0 (0)	3 (18)	2 (7)	1 (5)	9 (12)	6 (21)	4 (22)	2 (12)	4 (18)	3 (25)	43 (15)
Non-MBA graduate	2 (5)	1 (9)	2 (12)	0 (0)	0 (0)	4 (6)	1 (4)	1 (5)	5 (29)	1 (4)	1 (8)	18 (6)
Non-MBA graduate with prof.certification	13 (34)	4 (37)	4 (23)	10 (34)	7 (39)	21 (29)	5 (17)	6 (33)	4 (23)	9 (41)	2 (17)	85 (30)
MBA	3 (8)	2 (18)	1 (6)	4 (14)	2 (11)	6 (8)	2 (7)	3 (17)	1 (6)	2 (9)	1 (8)	27 (10)
MBA with prof. certification	0 (0)	0 (0)	1 (6)	0 (0)	0 (0)	1 (1)	1 (3) *	0 (0)	0 (0)	1 (5)	0 (0)	4 (1)
Total	38 (100)	11 (100)	17 (100)	29 (100)	18 (100)	73 (100)	29 (100)	18 (100)	17 (100)	22 (100)	12 (100)	284 (100)

The entries in each cell are "number of respondents" and ("column percentage") respectively.

WORK EXPERIENCE

Nearly 60% of budget managers have been in their current jobs for less than three years (Table 51, Question 43). Less than 20% of budget managers had held their jobs for over six years. These data suggest that a budget manager's job is being perceived as a stepping stone and not as a career. The only exception to this conclusion is the life insurance industry, where one-third of the firms have budget managers with over six years of experience in their current job. This poses an important question: Do the firms have a formal program to recruit, train, and develop budget managers? Firms without such programs are likely to experience some difficulty in replacing budget managers after they accept a different assignment.

Over 55% of the budget managers had worked with the current employer for over six years (Table 52, Question 43). Large manufacturing, utilities, and life insurance firms have a high proportion of managers with over 10 years of experience with the present employer.

About half the budget managers in diversified service, transportation, and diversified finance firms have less than seven years of experience in current or closely related industries (Table 53, Question 43). Budget managers in other industries have more work experience.

Nearly half the budget managers in several industries have over 13 years of experience in accounting/finance. Further, nearly 40% of budget managers have no nonfinancial experience (Table 54, Question 43). This may reflect a bias toward recruiting only persons with accounting/finance for the budget manager's job. Such a bias may be unfortunate, since a good budget manager should have excellent interpersonal, communication, and negotiation skills. Accounting/finance knowledge alone may not be sufficient, and the possibility of recruiting budget managers with other areas of specialization should be explored. A budget manager's job could also be used to provide a comprehensive experience to a manager being groomed for a senior management position.

Table 51
Number of Respondents by Industry and Work Experience of Budget Manager in the Current Job (Question 43)

Years in the Current Job	Commercial Banks	Diversified Financial	Diversified Service	Hospitals	Life Insurance	Large Manufacturing	Medium Manufacturing	Retailers/ Wholesalers	Transportation	Utilities	Miscellaneous	Total
0 - 1	9 (24)	4 (40)	7 (41)	8 (28)	2 (11)	22 (30)	6 (21)	5 (28)	4 (24)	6 (27)	2 (17)	75 (26)
2 - 3	13 (34)	1 (10)	4 (24)	9 (31)	4 (22)	27 (37)	11 (38)	3 (17)	5 (29)	8 (37)	4 (33)	89 (32)
4 - 6	13 (34)	3 (30)	2 (12)	7 (24)	6 (34)	16 (22)	5 (17)	6 (33)	6 (35)	4 (18)	3 (25)	71 (25)
Over 6	3 (8)	2 (20)	4 (23)	5 (17)	6 (33)	8 (11)	7 (24)	4 (22)	2 (12)	4 (18)	3 (25)	48 (17)
Total	38 (100)	10 (100)	17 (100)	29 (100)	18 (100)	73 (100)	29 (100)	18 (100)	17 (100)	22 (100)	12 (100)	283 (100)

The entries in each cell are "number of respondents" and ("column percentage") respectively.

Table 52
Number of Respondents by Industry and Work Experience of Budget Manager with the Current Employer (Question 43)

Year with the Current Employer	Commercial Banks	Diversified Financial	Diversified Service	Hospitals	Life Insurance	Large Manufacturing	Medium Manufacturing	Retailers/ Wholesalers	Transportation	Utilities	Miscellaneous	Total
0 – 3	8 (21)	2 (20)	4 (24)	15 (52)	1 (6)	13 (18)	10 (33)	4 (22)	3 (18)	2 (9)	4 (33)	66 (23)
4 – 6	10 (26)	2 (20)	7 (41)	7 (24)	4 (22)	7 (9)	6 (20)	5 (28)	4 (24)	3 (14)	4 (33)	59 (21)
7 – 10	13 (34)	2 (20)	1 (6)	5 (17)	2 (11)	18 (25)	7 (24)	4 (22)	6 (35)	5 (23)	3 (25)	66 (23)
Over 10	7 (19)	4 (40)	5 (29)	2 (7)	11 (61)	35 (48)	7 (23)	5 (28)	4 (23)	12 (54)	1 (9)	93 (33)
Total	38 (100)	10 (100)	17 (100)	29 (100)	18 (100)	73 (100)	30 (100)	18 (100)	17 (100)	22 (100)	12 (100)	284 (100)

The entries in each cell are "number of respondents" and ("column percentage") respectively.

Table 53
Number of Respondents by Industry and Work Experience of Budget Manager in Current or Closely Related Industries (Question 43)

Years of Experience	Commercial Banks	Diversified Financial	Diversified Service	Hospitals	Life Insurance	Large Manufacturing	Medium Manufacturing	Retailers/ Wholesalers	Transportation	Utilities	Miscellaneous	Total
0 – 6	8 (27)	4 (45)	10 (59)	10 (37)	1 (7)	11 (19)	8 (36)	1 (7)	7 (50)	5 (29)	4 (40)	69 (30)
7 – 10	15 (50)	1 (11)	1 (6)	9 (33)	2 (13)	17 (29)	6 (27)	4 (29)	5 (36)	4 (24)	2 (20)	66 (28)
11 – 18	5 (17)	2 (22)	3 (18)	7 (26)	8 (53)	18 (31)	3 (14)	6 (43)	2 (14)	4 (24)	2 (20)	60 (26)
Over 18	2 (6)	2 (22)	3 (17)	1 (4)	4 (27)	12 (21)	5 (23)	3 (21)	0 (0)	4 (23)	2 (20)	38 (16)
Total	30 (100)	9 (100)	17 (100)	27 (100)	15 (100)	58 (100)	22 (100)	14 (100)	14 (100)	17 (100)	10 (100)	233 (100)

The entries in each cell are "number of respondents" and ("column percentage") respectively.

Table 54
Number of Respondents by Industry and Work Experience of Budget Manager in Nonfinancial Areas (Question 43)

Years of Experience	Commercial Banks	Diversified Financial	Diversified Service	Hospitals	Life Insurance	Large Manufacturing	Medium Manufacturing	Retailers/ Wholesalers	Transportation	Utilities	Miscellaneous	Total
0	5 (33)	4 (50)	4 (57)	4 (36)	6 (67)	10 (32)	3 (30)	1 (20)	3 (60)	3 (27)	2 (29)	45 (38)
1 – 6	9 (60)	1 (13)	3 (43)	6 (54)	0 (0)	15 (49)	3 (30)	3 (60)	1 (20)	4 (37)	4 (57)	49 (41)
Over 6	1 (7)	3 (37)	0 (0)	1 (10)	3 (33)	6 (19)	4 (40)	1 (20)	1 (20)	4 (36)	1 (14)	25 (21)
Total	15 (100)	8 (100)	7 (100)	11 (100)	9 (100)	31 (100)	10 (100)	5 (100)	5 (100)	11 (100)	7 (100)	119 (100)

The entries in each cell are "number of respondents" and ("column percentage") respectively.

TIME ALLOCATION

Coordinating and preparing the budget, and monitoring performance against budget consumes a high proportion of a budget manager's time (Tables 55 and 56, Question 45). Budget managers spend a small proportion of their time in follow-up and corrective action (Table 57, Question 45). Apparently, the budget manager's role is being perceived as advisory, and corrective actions are taken by other line managers. There is a need to examine whether budget managers should play a more active role in follow-up and corrective action.

ROLE OF THE BUDGET MANAGER

The data suggest that budget managers are perceived as professionals with specialized financial expertise who spend the bulk of their time in coordinating budget preparation and in monitoring performance against budget. Budget managers are not taking an active part in follow-up and corrective action, presumably because they perceive their role to be advisory. Each firm should examine whether it has defined the budget manager's role appropriately.

Table 55
Number of Respondents by Industry and Percentage of Budget Manager's Time Spent in Coordinating and Preparing the Budget (Question 45)

Percentage of Time	Commercial Banks	Diversified Financial	Diversified Service	Hospitals	Life Insurance	Large Manu-facturing	Medium Manu-facturing	Retailers/ Wholesalers	Transporta-tion	Utilities	Miscella-neous	Total
0 – 20%	10 (22)	2 (22)	7 (47)	7 (28)	7 (39)	20 (28)	9 (31)	7 (41)	5 (31)	3 (14)	3 (60)	80 (29)
21 – 40%	17 (37)	3 (34)	3 (20)	5 (20)	7 (39)	27 (38)	11 (38)	5 (29)	8 (50)	10 (45)	1 (20)	97 (36)
41 – 60%	3 (6)	2 (22)	3 (20)	11 (44)	4 (22)	18 (25)	4 (14)	4 (24)	3 (19)	5 (23)	1 (20)	58 (21)
Over 60%	16 (35)	2 (22)	2 (13)	2 (8)	0 (0)	6 (9)	5 (17)	1 (6)	0 (0)	4 (18)	0 (0)	38 (14)
Total	46 (100)	9 (100)	15 (100)	25 (100)	18 (100)	71 (100)	29 (100)	17 (100)	16 (100)	22 (100)	5 (100)	273 (100)

The entries in each cell are "number of respondents" and ("column percentage" respectively.

Table 56
Number of Respondents by Industry and Percentage of Budget Manager's Time Spent in Monitoring Performance against Budget (Question 45)

Percentage of Time	Commercial Banks	Diversified Financial	Diversified Service	Hospitals	Life Insurance	Large Manu- facturing	Medium Manu- facturing	Retailers/ Wholesalers	Transporta- tion	Utilities	Miscella- neous	Total
0 – 20%	17 (49)	4 (45)	6 (38)	10 (40)	8 (45)	20 (28)	14 (50)	7 (41)	7 (44)	6 (27)	3 (60)	102 (39)
21 – 40%	12 (34)	2 (22)	7 (44)	13 (52)	6 (33)	32 (46)	7 (25)	10 (59)	7 (44)	11 (50)	0 (0)	107 (41)
41 – 60%	6 (17)	3 (33)	1 (6)	2 (8)	4 (22)	16 (23)	6 (21)	0 (0)	2 (12)	4 (18)	2 (40)	46 (18)
Over 60%	0 (0)	0 (0)	2 (12)	0 (0)	0 (0)	2 (3)	1 (4)	0 (0)	0 (0)	1 (5)	0 (0)	6 (2)
Total	35 (100)	9 (100)	16 (100)	25 (100)	18 (100)	70 (100)	28 (100)	17 (100)	16 (100)	22 (100)	5 (100)	261 (100)

The entries in each cell are "number of respondents" and ("column percentage") respectively.

Table 57
Number of Respondents by Industry and Percentage of Budget Manager's Time Spent in Follow-up and Corrective Action (Question 45)

Percentage of Time	Commercial Banks	Diversified Financial	Diversified Service	Hospitals	Life Insurance	Large Manufacturing	Medium Manufacturing	Retailers/ Wholesalers	Transportation	Utilities	Miscellaneous	Total
0 – 20%	24 (75)	7 (88)	9 (69)	18 (72)	12 (67)	49 (73)	16 (59)	11 (69)	10 (67)	13 (59)	4 (80)	173 (70)
21 – 40%	6 (19)	0 (0)	2 (16)	4 (16)	4 (22)	12 (18)	8 (30)	4 (25)	4 (27)	7 (32)	1 (20)	52 (21)
41 – 60%	1 (3)	1 (12)	2 (15)	3 (12)	2 (11)	6 (9)	3 (11)	1 (6)	1 (6)	2 (9)	0 (0)	22 (8)
Over 60%	1 (3)	0 (0)	0 (0)	0 (0)	0 (0)	0 (0)	0 (0)	0 (0)	0 (0)	0 (0)	0 (0)	1 (1)
Total	32 (100)	8 (100)	13 (100)	25 (100)	18 (100)	67 (100)	27 (100)	16 (100)	15 (100)	22 (100)	5 (100)	248 (100)

The entries in each cell are "number of respondents" and ("column percentage") respectively.

7

Changes in Budgetary Practices during the Period 1958–1984

Sord and Welsch published the results of a comprehensive study of budgetary practices in 1958. Although significant changes have taken place in the business environment since that time, the changes in budgetary practices had not been documented so far. This chapter compares and contrasts the findings of this study with those of Sord and Welsch.

PRESENCE OF A FORMAL BUDGET PROGRAM

Sord and Welsch reported that 89% of the respondents had a formal budget program. Currently 97% of the firms have a budget program (Table 8). Almost all firms use budgets, and the increased usage is probably because of the proven advantages of budgeting.

INDIVIDUALS OR GROUPS INVOLVED

Sord and Welsch found that in over 25% of the companies, the board of directors, executive committee, and management committee were involved in approving budgets. This study points out that these committees approve budgets less frequently (Table 9). Such a difference reflects a change in management philosophy toward deemphasizing the role of committees in making or approving decisions.

GOAL-SETTING PROCESS

The goal-setting process currently used is more centralized and top-down than that reported in the Sord and Welsch study. It is likely that the recessionary pressures during the period 1981-1984 may have persuaded several firms to opt for a more centralized budgetary process (Table 10).

REVIEW OF ANNUAL BUDGET

Monthly and quarterly reviews for possible revision of goals have increased considerably, and the net result is increased frequency of reviews for planning purposes (Table 14). Although frequent reviews will contribute to improved monitoring of operations, they may lead to an unintended focus on the short term. Further, a target that is revised too frequently will not generate commitment or motivation to achieve the goal.

MANAGEMENT VIEW OF BUDGETS

The proportion of managers who believe that budgets increase output and efficiency by exerting pressure on employees is significantly greater today (Table 20). Although the optimal amount of pressure to be applied is not known, the increasing trend toward applying pressure on managers is quite clear.

AREAS IN WHICH FORMAL PLANS OR BUDGETS ARE PREPARED

More target areas and a greater proportion of firms specifying their long-term goals for each target area are the observed changes (Questions 22 and 23). Widespread dissemination of various budgeting techniques is probably the reason.

FREQUENCY OF UPDATING LONG-RANGE PLANS

Long-range plans are updated each year by 85% of the firms, as opposed to 48% in 1958 (Question 23). Frequent updating of long-range plans may result in an unintended bias toward preparing long-range plans by mere extrapolation of short-term budgets.

TITLE OF THE LONG-RANGE PLANNER

The title of the person responsible for long-range planning suggests that the function is considered to be more important today and has been accorded a higher status within the organization (Question 23).

TYPES OF FORECASTS AND PROCEDURES USED

More types of forecasts and greater reliance on multiple procedures to develop such forecasts were observed by comparing the present study with that of Sord and Welsch (Question 27). Improved sources of business information and more efficient data-processing tools are primarily responsible for this change. Have we crossed the point beyond which additional information is counter productive? What should we do when different types of forecasts or those prepared from alternative data yield widely varying results? These are some questions that should be answered by firms that are contemplating the introduction of improved forecasting methods.

USE OF FORMAL APPROACHES

Budget manuals are being used by 64% of the firms compared with the 49% reported by Sord and Welsch (Question 30). However, the proportion of control reports covering the current performance of a manager that are matched with his or her organizational authority and responsibility has dropped significantly in the category "fully," from 56% to 18% (Question 32). The increased gap between responsibility structure and performance reports is indeed a matter of grave concern. An alternative explanation is that today's organizations are more complex; therefore, achieving a fit between the responsibility structure and performance reports is difficult.

STANDARDS FOR REVENUES AND EXPENSES

Historical revenue and cost data are being used more frequently than in the past (Question 33). Although budgets are emphasized more in measuring, controlling or evaluating current sales or service revenues, they are used less frequently to monitor and control revenues (Question 34). The heavy emphasis on historical data is based on the implicit assumption that past performance is nearly optimal. Wherever this assumption is not valid, the emphasis on past data is ill advised.

BUDGETARY PRACTICES

The proportion of firms using flexible budgets, classifying expenses into controllable and noncontrollable categories, and subdividing budgets by product lines has come down since the Sord and Welsch study (Question 34). This is counter intuitive because these practices are recommended in all introductory textbooks in management accounting, and we have much more sophisticated data-processing facilities. Each firm should periodically examine whether the basic components of a responsibility accounting system are present in the organization.

Where a report shows a significant deviation from the company's standards of performance or budget, it is handled by greater reliance on written explanations (Question 39). Simultaneously, one finds that the proportion of firms using discussions with immediate superior has dropped from 66% in the Sord and Welsch study to 56% reported in this study. Informal processes are apparently giving way to formal procedures and processes.

This pattern is also noticed in the manner in which companies convey to each manager or supervisor a clear understanding of the responsibilities of his or her department or profit center (Question 35). Formal conferences are emphasized more and informal conferences are used less frequently today in communicating the responsibilities to senior and middle managers. The primary communication process used for defining the responsibilities of senior managers is formal conferences. Informal conferences are used more frequently at the middle and lower management levels. The use of a copy of the operating plan to define budget responsibilities has decreased, especially at the lower management levels. These changes are significant. However, we do not know whether the changes have led to improved communication of managerial responsibilities.

TITLE OF THE BUDGET MANAGER

The Sord and Welsch study found that in nearly two-thirds of the firms the corporate controller was the primary person responsible for preparing budgets (Question 43). The respondents to this study report that in 56% of the firms the person has the title of budget director, and only 20% of the firms report that the corporate controller is the primary person responsible for preparing budgets. The corresponding numbers for the Sord and Welsch study are 16% and 63%, respectively. Thus, there seems to be increased awareness of the need for recognizing the importance of budgeting by assigning a person with the sole responsibility of expressing the objectives and goals of various organizational subunites in financial terms.

BUDGETARY EFFECTIVENESS

The previous comparisons demonstrate that significant changes in budgetary practices have taken place. Some of them, such as assigning a person to the primary responsibility of preparing budgets, are welcome changes that will improve budgetary effectiveness. Although the two studies do not provide complete information linking budget practices to effectiveness, the following changes may have adversely affected the performance in the industry:

1. Decreased emphasis on the use of committees, informal processes, and discussions of variances with immediate superiors
2. Increased frequency of reviews for possible revision of goals

3. Increasing trend toward a top-down process and toward increasing the pressure on managers during budgetary processes

4. Tendency to use more sources of information and more analytical tools to prepare forecasts, possibly leading to conflicting conclusions

5. Increased reliance on historical data in establishing standards

6. Increase in the misfit between responsibility structure and performance reporting system

7. Decreased use of simple yet proven techniques of management accounting, such as use of flexible budgets, classifying costs into controllable and noncontrollable categories, and subdividing the budget by product lines

8. Increased reliance on persons with specialized training and work experience, primarily in accounting and finance, to be appointed as budget managers; and treating a budget manager's job as a stepping-stone and not as a career

It is not difficult to overcome these deficiencies or reverse the undesirable trends. Lack of awareness and absence of a commitment to optimize budgetary effectiveness are probably the two major explanations for the presence of the imperfections just listed. The final chapter of this book provides some specific action plans to improve budgetary effectiveness.

8

Company Characteristics and Budgetary Practices

Budgetary control systems should be tailored to the needs of each organization. Budgetary practices should be carefully selected so that they fit with relevant situational factors. This chapter describes the relationships among six company characteristics and budgetary practices. These relationships were explored by examining cross tabulations of each company characteristic with each budgetary practice and selecting those relationships which were significant at the 1%, 5%, or 10% level. The level of significance for each relationship is presented within parentheses. The lower the percentage within parentheses, the more significant the relationship. Only statistically significant relationships are discussed in this chapter.

The six company characteristics examined are

1. *Size* as measured by number of employees
2. *Diversification* as measured by number of two-digit Standard Industrial Classification codes (SIC) for the products or services offered by the company
3. *Company strategy* based on responses to Question 1.

4. *Rate of change in the business environment* based on the sum of scores for 10 items in Question 2

5. *Level of interdependence* based on level of intracompany sales as a percentage of total company sales (Question 3)

6. *Type of industry:* the respondents were classified into manufacturing, nonfinancial services, and financial services

The relationships among these six characteristics and budgetary practices are discussed here.

SIZE

Larger firms adopt the following practices more frequently than smaller firms:

• Review annual budget for possible revision of goals, for evaluation purposes (1%)

• Use budgets for compensating managers (1%), educating managers (1%), communicating the priorities established by top management (1%), planning (5%) and evaluating managers (5%)

• Use formal procedures to schedule and monitor the preparation of budgets (1%) and to evaluate the extent to which budgets were being prepared and used effectively by managers (1%)

• Use relatively more sophisticated budgetary practices such as attempting to match the control reports covering the current performance of a manager with his or her organizational authority and responsibility (5%) or subdividing budget by product lines (10%) and by major subunits of the company (10%)

• Avoid dysfunctional behaviors such as deferring a needed expenditure (1%), accelerating a sale (1%), getting approvals after money was spent (5%), and accelerating a capital expenditure because money was available (5%)

• Assign a senior position and title to the budget manager (1%)

DIVERSIFICATION

Companies with a greater degree of diversification use the following budgetary practices more frequently than the less diversified firms:

- Review budgets for possible revision of goals for planning purposes (5%)
- Use budgets for compensating managers (1%), evaluating managers (1%), educating managers (1%), planning (5%), and motivating managers (5%)
- Use formal procedures to evaluate budgetary effectiveness (1%)
- Use relatively more sophisticated budgetary practices such as preparing contingency plans (10%), using rolling budgets (10%), and subdividing budgets by product lines (10%)
- Avoid engaging in dysfunctional behaviors such as accelerating a sale (1%) and shifting funds between accounts (10%)
- Use performance reports to analyze expenses (1%), hold discussions of deviations (1%) from budgets, and use oral explanations (10%) whenever a significant deviation from the company's standards is noticed

COMPANY STRATEGY

Growth-oriented firms use the following budgetary practices more frequently than relatively stable firms:

- Use fewer and less difficult targets (1%)
- Use budgets for motivating (1%), evaluating (1%), compensating (1%) managers, planning (5%), and communicating the priorities of the top management (1%)
- Subdivide budgets by major subunits of the company and use techniques such as Critical Path Method to schedule and monitor budget preparation
- Avoid dysfunctional behaviors such as shifting funds between accounts (1%) and accelerating a sale (1%)

RATE OF CHANGE IN THE BUSINESS ENVIRONMENT

Firms with a higher rate of change adopt the following practices more frequently than relatively stable firms:

- Use budgets for communication (10%) and coordination (10%)
- Review annual budget for possible revision of goals for planning purposes (5%)

- Use Gantt charts to schedule and monitor budget preparation
- Avoid using budget games such as accelerating a sale (1%) or shifted funds between accounts (10%)

LEVEL OF INTERDEPENDENCE

Firms having a high level of interdependence engage in the following budgetary practices more frequently:

- Use budgets for motivating (1%), communicating (1%), evaluating, (5%) and coordinating (10%)
- Review annual budget for possible revision of goals for planning purposes (5%) and adopt a formal process for evaluating the effectiveness of budgeting (10%)
- Break long-term plans into short-term programs or projects (10%) and require projects to be approved prior to the commencement of the budget cycle (5%)
- Use sophisticated techniques such as flexible budgeting (5%), rolling budgets (5%), contingency plans (1%), subdividing budget by product lines (5%), and classifying expenses into controllable and noncontrollable categories (5%)
- Practice fewer budget games such as accelerating a sale (1%), deferring a needed expenditure (10%), and accelerating capital expenditures (10%)

TYPE OF INDUSTRY

The firms were classified into three broad groups: manufacturing, nonfinancial service, and financial service industries. Manufacturing firms at one end of the spectrum have higher capital intensity, clearer standards for processing inputs, and concrete measures of efficiency and effectiveness. Nonfinancial and financial service firms have relatively lower capital intensity, less clear standards for processing resource inputs, and fuzzy measures of efficiency and effectiveness.

This section describes the observed relationship between industry category and budgetary practices. Manufacturing firms use the following practices more frequently than nonfinancial service companies, which in turn adopt these practices more frequently than financial service organizations:

- Use budgets for planning (10%), evaluating managers (5%), compensating managers (1%), and educating managers (10%)
- Have a higher proportion of managers participate in both long-range planning and budgeting processes (1%) and require approval of projects before the commencement of the budget cycle (5%)
- Use sophisticated budgeting techniques such as flexible budgets (1%), subdividing the budget by product lines (1%), using detailed and comprehensive procedures for a high proportion of budgeting activities (10%), and using performance reports that matched with managerial authority and responsibility (5%)
- Engage in budget games such as accelerating a sale (1%), using contract labor to stay within headcount limits (5%), shifting funds between accounts to avoid budget overruns (10%), and deferring a needed expenditure (10%)

CONCLUSION

The primary finding reported in this chapter is that situational factors do have an impact on budgetary practices. Managers should therefore identify relevant situational factors and take them into consideration while designing and using budgetary controls. The first five situational factors could be related to a comprehensive measure which we shall refer to as "degree of complexity of the organization." A summary of the impact of the first five situational factors on the degree of complexity follows:

1. *Size:* Larger organizations are more complex.
2. *Diversification:* Organizations that are more diversified are more complex.
3. *Company Strategy:* Firms that have a growth strategy are more complex than those which are primarily in stable businesses. Growth-oriented companies which frequently acquire and divest divisions are the most complex.
4. *Rate of Change:* Companies experiencing a high rate of change are more complex than those operating in stable business environments.
5. *Level of Interdependence:* Firms with highly interdependent divisions are more complex than those with independent divisions.

The findings reported in this chapter suggest that complex firms use more sophisticated budgetary controls. This is consistent with our expectations because a complex organization is more difficult to manage, and tools used in managing complex organizations should therefore be more sophisticated. Based on the analysis of survey data, we can conclude that an organization which is characterized by a high degree of complexity should do the following:

- Plan to use its budgets for a variety of purposes such as planning, coordinating various activities, motivating, evaluating, and compensating managers, as well as for communicating organizational priorities and educating managers
- Build strong linkages between long-term plans and budgets through managers participating in both processes and by breaking long-term plans into short-term programs or projects and by requiring approvals prior to the commencement of the budget cycle
- Review budgets for possible revision of goals, either for planning or evaluation purposes
- Use detailed and comprehensive procedures for a high proportion of budgeting activities and match control reports with a manager's authority and responsibility
- Use techniques such as Gantt charts or Critical Path Method for scheduling and monitoring the preparation of budgets
- Use simple yet effective techniques such as flexible budgeting, classifying expenses into controllable and noncontrollable categories, preparation of contingency plans and rolling budgets, and subdividing budget by product lines and by major subunits of a company
- Use reports comparing actual current performance with standards of performance or budget objectives prepared for each department or profit center
- Anticipate more budget games and take steps to minimize such dysfunctional behavior

Variations in budgetary practices across different industries are quite significant. Such disparity suggests that managers should attempt to improve the effectiveness of their budgetary controls by selectively adopting budgetary practices used by comparable firms and comparable industries.

9

Budgetary Practices in Successful Firms

Managers are interested in finding out whether budgetary practices in successful firms differ from those in other firms. This chapter identifies the specific practices which are used by the more successful firms. Four measures of performance were used:

- Financial performance (Question 4)
- Self-ratings of budgetary effectiveness (Question 42)
- Return on equity
- Price-to-earnings ratio

Data for the last two measures were obtained from financial directories. The level of statistical significance is indicated in parentheses.

BUDGETARY PRACTICES AND PERFORMANCE

- Number of nonfinancial targets (Question 8) used is positively related to both financial performance (10%) and budgetary effectiveness (1%).

- Difficulty of budgetary targets (Question 9) is negatively correlated with financial performance (10%), budgetary effectiveness (1%), and return on equity (5%). In other words, firms having more difficult budgetary targets are poor performers.

- Review of budget for possible revision of goals for evaluation purposes (Question 10) has a favorable influence on return on equity (1%).

- Use of budgets for planning, coordination, motivation, evaluation, compensation of managers, communication, and education of managers (Question 13) has a positive impact on financial performance (1% to 10%) and budgetary effectiveness (1%).

- The practice of dividing long-term plans into medium-term or short-term programs or projects (Question 25) is associated with better financial performance (5%), budgetary effectiveness (10%), and return on equity (10%).

- Tightness of linkage between the numbers used in the budget and the first year of long-range plan (Question 24) has a favorable impact on budgetary effectiveness (5%).

- Use of techniques for scheduling and monitoring the preparation of budgets (Question 29) has a favorable impact on budgetary effectiveness (5%) and price-to-earnings ratio (10%).

- Use of a formal procedure to evaluate the extent to which budgets were being prepared and used effectively (Question 30) has a positive influence on budgetary effectiveness (1%) and return on equity (10%).

- The proportion of budgeting activities for which detailed, comprehensive procedures (Question 31) are used is associated positively with budgetary effectiveness (1%).

- The greater the proportion of control reports that matched organizational authority and responsibility of managers (Question 32), the better the reported financial performance (10%) and budgetary effectiveness (1%).

- Use of sophisticated budgeting techniques (Questions 34, 36, and 37) has a favorable impact on financial performance (10%), budgetary effectiveness (1% to 5%), and return on equity (10%). These techniques include the use of flexible budgets, contingency plans, rolling budgets, and subdividing budgets by organizational subunits.

- Requiring written explanations for deviations from company's budget (Question 39, 10%) or asking managers to indicate corrective action taken (5%) has a favorable impact on budgetary effectiveness.

- The practice of engaging in budget games such as getting approvals after spending money, accelerating a sale, deferring a needed expenditure, or accelerating a capital expenditure (Question 41) has an unfavorable influence on financial performance (1% to 10%) and budgetary effectiveness (5%).

- Assigning a higher-level title to the budget manager (10%) and hiring a person with considerable experience in accounting/finance (5%) is associated with better financial performance (Question 43).

- Spending more time in follow-up and corrective action has a favorable impact on return on equity.

All the relationships described here are associative in nature. They do not describe a cause-and-effect relationship. However, logical reasoning and earlier studies of some of these variables suggest that adoption of the previously cited practices will result in improved performance.

It is worth noting that many of the budgetary practices just discussed are also found in relatively more complex firms (see Chapter 8). Absence of these budgetary practices could therefore lead to poor performance in any firm, especially in a complex company. A good strategy for any company interested in improving its performance would be to emulate the budgetary practices used by an effective organization of comparable complexity in its own industry.

GUIDELINES TO IMPROVE
BUDGETARY PERFORMANCE

These results suggest that some budgeting practices are more desirable than others. However, these practices frequently cost more. Complex organizations cannot avoid incurring the cost because, unless they have a sophisticated budgetary process, their performance will suffer. Simpler firms have to carefully examine whether the benefits derived from a superior budgetary control system would justify its cost. Guidelines for designing budgetary controls for an organization of medium complexity are summarized here:

- Assess the degree of complexity of the firm by using five-point scale for each of the six company characteristics discussed in chapter 8. As a rule of thumb, a score of 18 to 24 would indicate medium complexity.

Firms having a score higher than 24 should use a comprehensive budgetary control system.

- Establish long-term objectives and goals using a bottom-up process. Gain commitment to the organizational goals by involving all key managers and by using a participative process.

- Establish linkages between the long-term plans and short-term budgets through people (managers participating in both processes) and through the use of identical numbers for a specific year in both long- and short-term plans.

- Plan to use budgetary controls for a variety of purposes. The more you expect from your budgetary control system, the more you will get out of it.

- Design the information system such that flexible budgets could be prepared, expenses could be classified into controllable and noncontrollable categories, and budgets could be subdivided by product lines or by organizational subunits. Consider preparing either contingency plans or rolling budgets on a regular basis.

- Periodically assess the effectiveness of your budgetary control system and decide whether you have the right person holding the budget manager's position.

- Develop procedures wherever possible, and present them clearly in a budget manual.

- Ensure that there is a fit between the control reports used and the responsibility and authority of managers.

- Examine variations from budgets by discussing with the managers and by requiring oral or written explanations.

- Periodically monitor the extent to which budget games are being played. Beyond a certain level, budget games could cause some permanent damage to the organization. Budget games usually indicate that the managers do not consider budgetary targets to be reasonable. If budget games are present, determine why managers do not consider budgetary targets to be acceptable, and take remedial action.

10

Implications for Managers and Academics

As the most recent and comprehensive study of budget practices in the United States, this study has helped answer the basic question: How do managers prepare and use budgets? Although this is a simple question, it has not been addressed for many years. An earlier comprehensive study of budgeting dates back to 1958. In addition to describing current budgetary practices based on a representative cross section of companies in nine industries, this study describes how budgetary practices are related to company characteristics and to company performance. This chapter presents a conceptual model of effective planning and control systems and discusses the implications of this study for both practitioners and academics.

A CONCEPTUAL MODEL OF EFFECTIVE PLANNING AND CONTROL SYSTEMS

The conceptual model discussed in this section is based on an interdisciplinary framework. The model is based on the combined perspectives of accounting, organizational behavior, and management policy. Although the model describes an optimal planning and control system, it can be used for designing new budgetary control systems, for diagnosing weaknesses in existing budgetary control systems, or for developing an action plan to improve existing controls. The results of this study validate several predictions of the model.

The model considers budgetary controls to be linked to specific organizational subsystems. A schematic diagram of the model, presented here, is followed by a description of the components of the model as well as some guidelines on how to use the model to improve budgeting in any company.

A Conceptual Model of Effective Planning and Control Systems

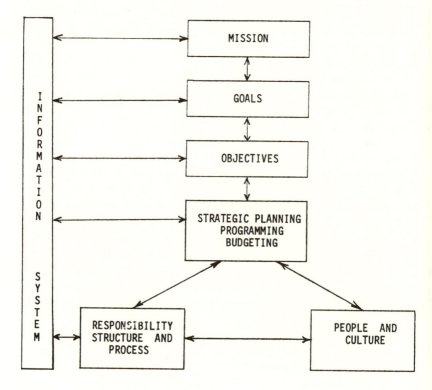

The components of the model and their interrelationships in an effective company follow:

Mission

Effective firms use a mission statement to communicate their values and beliefs. A mission statement is timeless and lays the foundation for the company and its purpose. The senior managers of the firm generate a commitment toward the mission statement through their actions and decisions. Whenever there are conflicts among the components of a mission statement, the relative priorities should be clarified by the senior managers.

Goals

Goals have a long-term horizon and specify a major task for the entire company. A goal poses a challenge to all the employees in the firm. A firm which has generated a high level of commitment toward its mission is in a better position to set a goal and obtain the commitment of the people to work toward the goal. A goal usually has an intentional fuzzy deadline and output specification. Often goals involve tasks which have not been attempted before. Goals motivate employees by providing them with an opportunity to be a member of a team working on an ambitious project. "To set up a semiconductor factory in outer space by the end of the 1980s" is an example of a goal.

Objectives

Objectives are more specific than goals and assign the responsibility to a specific person, department, or division. Objectives have a medium- to long-term time horizon. Unless there is a commitment toward goals, it is difficult to obtain commitment of managers to the objectives. Objectives have specific deadlines and broad output specifications. "To prepare a list of alternative semiconductor products to be manufactured in outer space and to develop project proposals for a handful of selected products by the end of 1988" is an example of an objective.

Strategic Planning, Programming, and Budgeting

These three components of Integrated Planning and Control Systems (IPCS) help achieve the objectives with the help of strategies, programs, and budgets. A strategy usually defines the scope of the business by specifying product characteristics, target market, niche in the market in terms of price and quality, and finally how the company plans to compete in the market. While objectives specify what a firm wants to do, strategy specifies how to achieve the objectives. A program is a group of interrelated activities associated with the implementation of one or more elements of a strategy. During the programming phase, discrete programs are identified, developed into proposals, and ranked. For each of the selected programs, resources needed for each year or part thereof are identified through the budgetary process. Effective firms generate commitment to objectives, strategies, programs, and budgets by developing them through a bottom-up process.

Responsibility Structure and Process

Once the strategy has been specified, the tasks associated with strategy implementation should be identified, and an organization structure should be designed to translate the strategy into action. In addition to designing the organization chart, the process by which the responsibilities are identified, grouped, and assigned to managers should be implemented carefully. Although such a process cannot be designed fully, senior managers can influence or guide the process through their participation.

People and Culture

Each firm should try to attract people whose values and beliefs are in alignment with its mission statement. The process by which strategies, programs, and budgets are formulated and implemented should help create a culture within the firm that reinforces the values and beliefs stressed in the mission statement.

Information System

Information is an important resource for the entire company. By providing relevant inputs during every stage of the planning and control process, a good information system facilitates the process of translating fuzzy and qualitative mission statements into specific financial targets during budgeting. Information systems also provide comparisons of actuals with targets as well as analyses to evaluate periodically the appropriateness of budgetary targets, or even the objectives. Good information systems permit the managers to conduct a variety of "what if" types of analyses during the planning cycle.

HOW TO USE THE MODEL TO DESIGN EFFECTIVE BUDGETARY CONTROLS

The model suggests that budgetary controls do not exist in isolation and are linked to other components of a planning and control system. The design of budgetary controls should therefore be accompanied by the design of other components of planning and control systems.

The model suggests that long-term plans should be prepared before short-term plans are undertaken. Thus, defining the mission statement facilitates the preparation of goals, and a clear set of goals is needed for establishing meaningful objectives. Once the objectives are finalized, strategies, programs, and budgets are prepared in a chronological sequence, and an appropriate responsibility structure and process, as well as people and culture components, have to be designed and implemented. These chronological linkages are helpful in establishing realistic targets during each stage of the planning and control process.

It is also desirable to have some people participate in two successive components of the planning and control system. For example, by having some common members in the committees for goals and objectives, the assumptions, values, and criteria used in finalizing goals will be taken into account while preparing the objectives. This type of linkage between the long and the short term could be called "people linkage."

A third type of linkage is created by ensuring that the language, numbers, and formats used in each component of the planning and control system can be dovetailed with the next component. This type of content linkage helps managers understand how their activities contribute to achieving the overall corporate objectives. Ideally, the content of the long-term and short-term plans should include both financial and nonfinancial information so that meaningful linkages could be built between the two plans.

In order to motivate managers to be actively involved in the planning process, and to commit themselves to the plan targets, the strategies, programs, and budgets should match the responsibility structure and process of the firm. It is also necessary to staff the company with the right kind of people and create a desirable organizational culture within the firm. Hence, considerable care should be taken in recruiting, training, and developing the employees. Only those employees whose beliefs and values are congruent with those of the company are likely to make significant contributions to the company.

The information system should be treated as a valuable resource in preparing plans, in monitoring actuals with plan targets, and in taking corrective action. Feedback information comparing actuals with targets could be called Level I feedback. To maximize the benefits of Level I feedback, the information should be classified in accordance with the responsibility structure (e.g., by division or by product line), as well as into controllable and noncontrollable categories. The impact of changes in levels of activity should be isolated by using flexible budgets. After managers understand the performance of various subunits of the company, Level II feedback should be used to examine the appropriateness of the plan targets and the budgetary processes. Level II analysis should preferably be undertaken each year before the commencement of the planning process.

Level III feedback should be provided to senior managers once every three to five years to examine whether the goals, objectives, and strategies established by the firm were appropriate and whether any changes should be made. The use of all three levels of feedback will ensure that the managers learn from both successes and failures and will ultimately lead to optimal company performance. Willingness of the top management to adopt all three levels of feedback is also likely to foster an organizational culture in which people are interested in receiving both favorable and unfavorable feedback. These managers are more likely to take calculated risks and learn from the outcomes. By focusing the attention of managers on learning from the planning and control system, the pressure on managers to play budget games is decreased.

This planning and control system will work only if the managers are evaluated using multiple criteria including short- and long-term financial targets, productivity goals, market share, product quality, technological position, human resources development, relations with suppliers and customers, and social responsibility. Although subjective assessments and detailed discussions will be needed, this type of performance evaluation system will motivate managers to use planning and control systems as the means to achieve goals, instead of treating plan targets as the ultimate goal.

While attempting to improve an existing budgetary control system, it may not be feasible for a company to implement all of the recommendations offered here. A planned approach to introducing changes is needed. There are several similarities between the previously stated guidelines and the budgetary practices of financially successful firms described in Chapter 9. This survey of current budgetary practices therefore supports the major postulates of the conceptual model presented in this chapter.

IMPLICATIONS FOR MANAGERS

This study has documented variations in budgetary practices both within an industry and across industries. Although most firms use budgets, some budgetary practices are associated with better performance. This study provides some suggestions (chapters 8 and 9) to improve effectiveness of budgetary controls. By implementing these recommendations, the performance of any organization can be improved. The conceptual model presented earlier and the guidelines based on it can be used to identify the changes needed in improving budgetary controls in a firm, as well as to specify the sequence in which the changes should be introduced. The questionnaire and summary results presented in Appendix I can serve as a diagnostic checklist to identify major deficiencies in a firm's budgetary control system.

A major conclusion of the study is that budgeting is a self-fulfilling prophecy. Companies that believe that budgeting is a powerful tool take the trouble to design the controls to match organizational needs, use it effectively, and achieve high levels of performance. In contrast, firms that do not believe in budgets pay lip service to design and use of budgetary controls, literally encourage their managers to play budget games, and finally blame the budget for the poor results. Thus, the first step to improving budgetary controls in any firm is to create a climate of trust in which everyone acknowledges the importance of budgeting and makes a commitment to make budgets work. Such a climate is necessary to ensure that the procedures and techniques used in budgeting can do the job.

Budgeting is like a surgeon's knife. In the skilled hands of a surgeon with the necessary training and experience, it can save the life of a patient. However, in the hands of an untrained person, that same knife could be a dangerous tool, especially if the environmental conditions are unsatisfactory. A budget can be effectively used, abused, incorrectly used, or not used at all. Managers need to decide what they want to do with budgets and then work toward achieving their expectations of budgets.

The vast amounts of resources, especially human resources invested in budgetary processes, suggest that managers consider budgetary processes to be useful. It is hoped that this study will contribute to improving budgetary effectiveness in any industry.

IMPLICATIONS FOR ACADEMICS

Budgeting is usually taught in managerial and cost accounting courses. These courses emphasize the procedural aspects of budgeting and pay lip service to behavioral aspects of budgeting. The teaching materials used are often outdated. This study will help instructors by providing data on current budgetary practices.

Academic research in budgeting is frequently based on analyses of two variables at a time and usually ignores other intervening variables. The findings of this study, together with the conceptual model, can be used to generate hypotheses involving three or more variables for future research. The findings on the relationships between situational factors and budgetary practices, and between budgetary practices and performance, can be transformed into specific hypotheses for further research. The data base generated by the study includes the responses from 402 firms and represents the most comprehensive data ever created on budget practices. It could be used as a powerful resource for generating and testing hypotheses.

Appendix I

A Summary of Questionnaire Responses

NATIONAL ASSOCIATION OF ACCOUNTANTS

A STUDY OF
THE STATE OF THE ART OF
BUDGET PRACTICES IN U.S. FIRMS

SAMPLE SIZE=402
(Frequency Distribution)

PART I: COMPANY CHARACTERISTICS

1. Which of the following terms best describes the strategic mission of your company? (Circle one number.)

Growth through acquisitions	16
Growth from within	107
Selective growth, primarily through acquisitions	65
Selective growth, primarily from within	175
Maintain operations/generate cash flow	31
Shrinking Operations	5

2. We would like to get a feel for how much change is going on in various segments of your company's business environment. Using the past three years as a point of reference, please rate each of the following items according to the rate of change you think has been occurring in it. (Circle one number in each row.)

	not applicable	no change	slight change	moderate change	considerable change	constant change
a. Product/Service characteristics	6	34	72	112	120	48
b. Market Demand	1	10	83	135	140	29
c. Distribution Network	37	65	119	89	70	14
d. Industry pricing patterns	18	17	75	122	126	37
e. Competitor's strategies						
f. Technical developments relevant to company's businesses	12	35	99	102	105	42
g. Production processes .	53	55	118	108	47	11
h. Government's economic policies & regulations .	4	37	96	86	101	71
i. Labor union's actions .	115	103	107	47	18	4
j. Human resources of the company	2	31	140	153	60	8
k. Availability of raw materials and other resources	93	103	91	58	25	14

3. Please indicate the approximate level of intra-company sales as a percentage of total company sales. (Check one box.)

122 0%   166 1-5%   43 6-10%   25 11-20%

24 21-40%   6 41-60%   4 Over 60%

4. Which of the following terms best describes your company's overall financial performance during the past three years? (Circle one number.)

a. Losing money 29

b. About break-even 26

c. Profitable, but less so than comparable companies 126

d. More profitable than comparable companies 216

5. Does your company have a formal budget program (profit planning or equivalent) for a period of one year or less?

388 Yes   12 No

If yes, please indicate the length of period:

5 3 months 11 6 months 352 12 months
10 Other (Please specify.) _____ months

If no to Question 5, please describe briefly the mechanism/s used by your company to monitor its overall performance.

_____

_____

> IF NO TO QUESTION 5, PLEASE DO NOT ANSWER THE REMAINING QUESTIONS. MAIL THIS QUESTIONNAIRE TO THE ADDRESS GIVEN AT THE END OF THE QUESTIONNAIRE. THANK YOU FOR YOUR COOPERATION.

PART II: MANAGEMENT PHILOSOPHY

6. What individuals or groups are involved in formally approving the budget for the company as a whole? (Please check one or more boxes applicable.)

☐ Board of Directors 229   ☐ Financial Vice President 225
☐ Executive Committee 114   ☐ Controller 167
☐ Chairman of the Board 213   ☐ Management Committee 85
☐ President 290   ☐ Planning Committee 32
☐ Executive Vice President 155 ☐ Budget Committee 52
                    ☐ Other (Specify.) _____ 18

7. In general, how are specific budgets or goals established? (Check one box only.)

25 ☐ Goals and objectives are established exclusively by members of higher management without consultation with subordinate levels of management.

76 ☐ Goals and objectves are developed by higher levels of management and are presented to subordinate levels of management for their consideration and comment prior to final adoption.

280 ☐ Subordinate levels of management are requested to submit goals and objectives relating to their particular function for review and final approval by higher levels of management.

13 ☐ Other. (Specify.) _____

_____

_____

8. Does your company usually establish specific non-financial budgetary targets for its managers in any of the following areas? (Check one box in each row.)

	Non-financial targets are used	
	Yes	No
a. New product/service development	225	154
b. Quality of product/service	254	124
c. Market Share	190	184
d. Customer relations	206	167
e. Relationships with suppliers	115	239
f. Productivity	276	101
g. Human Resources Development	232	146
h. Employee attitudes	144	221
i. Public responsibility	145	214
j. Balance between short- and long-range goals	187	173
k. Other (Specify.) _____	4	65

9. Using the past three years as a point of reference, please rate the extent of difficulty in achieving the financial targets used in your budgets? (Circle one number.)

Almost impossible	28
Challenging	201
Slightly beyond our reach	72
Just right	64
Relatively easy	24

10. (a.) Do you use two separate budgets, one for planning and coordination purposes, and the other for evaluation purposes? (Circle one number.)

Two separate budgets are used	28
Only one budget is prepared and it is used for planning, coordination and evaluation	294
Only one budget is prepared and it is used for evaluation purposes	21
Only one budget is prepared and it is used for planning and coordination purposes	50

(b.) How frequently do you review your annual budget for possible revision of goals, either for planning or evaluation purposes? (Circle one number each column.)

	Reviewed for	
	Planning purposes	Evaluation purposes
1. Never reviewed	25	59
2. Monthly	120	125
3. Quarterly	159	105
4. Semi-annually	49	43
5. Other (Specify.)		
	27	33

11. Please indicate which of the following statements best characterizes the types of information that, in your opinion, higher level managers in your company seem to focus on when assessing and evaluating organizational subunits. (Check one number.)

a. They seem to focus primarily on quantitative data; their focus on qualitative data is marginal 42

b. While they focus on both quantitative and qualitative data, more importance is given to quantitative data 208

c. They seem to focus almost equally on quantitative and qualitative data 102

d. While they focus on both quantitative and qualitative data, more importance is given to qualitative data 37

e. They seem to focus primarily on qualitative data; their focus on quantitative data is marginal 5

12. Does your company use computers for the following purposes?

a. Analysis of economic data ...223Yes 167No

b. Preparation of
long-range forecasts 291Yes 100No

c. Preparation of
long-range financial plans 312Yes 81No

d. Preparation of budgets 378Yes 16No

e. Preparation of
performance reports 356Yes 38No

13. To what extent do higher level managers in your company use budgets for the following purposes? (Circle one number in each row.)

	Not used	Small extent	Some extent	Mod. extent	Great extent	No Basis for an opinion
a. Planning	4	15	49	125	199	0
b. Coordinating various activities	5	43	97	134	92	18
c. Motivating managers	13	27	78	129	137	6
d. Evaluating managers	13	34	73	130	137	6
e. Compensating managers	47	45	83	88	124	6
f. Educating and developing managers	42	92	126	88	27	18
g. Communicating the priorities established by top management	11	32	84	110	155	1

14. Which of the views indicated below is most expressive of your top management view of budgets or standards of performance as control devices? (Check one box.)

48 They represent procedures which can be used effectively to exert pressure on subordinates, thereby improving efficiency and output.

232 They represent procedures which should be used to motivate subordinates to increase output and improve efficiency through participation in managerial planning and control.

53 They represent procedures which do motivate subordinates but primarily increase efficiency and output through pressure on subordinates.

53 They represent procedures which do exert some pressure on subordinates but primarily increase efficiency through motivation of employees

15. (a) Approximately what proportion of your company's higher level corporate managers have at least three years of education or work experience in accounting/finance? Check this box ☐ if you have no basis for an opinion.   103

   2 0%   95 1-10%   57 11-20%   52 21-30%
  23 31-40% 20 41-60% 14 61-80%   21 Over 80%

(b) How many employees (full time equivalent) at the corporate headquarters spend their time partly or fully in preparing budgets or performance reports? _____ Check this box ☐ if you have no basis for an opinion.   67

   Range 0 – 200 = 293

16. How frequently do corporate managers formally meet with lower level managers to discuss budget related matters? (Circle one number.)

Weekly	6	Semi-annually	30
Monthly	178	Annually	36
Quarterly	116	Other (Specify.)	
		_____	25

17. A profit center can be defined as any fairly independent organizational unit accountable separately for its performance, for which some measure of profit is determined periodically. Usually a profit center has its own manufacturing facilities and/or its own marketing department. It may be called a "division," "department," "branch," or "subsidiary" in your company. Approximately how many such profit centers report directly to either corporate- or group-level managers?

Number of Profit Centers

a. Domestic and within 50 miles of
   corporate headquarters .... _____
b. Domestic and more than 50 miles away ..... _____
c. Outside the United States .... _____

IF YOUR COMPANY IS NOT DIVIDED INTO PROFIT CENTERS, PLEASE CHECK THIS BOX ☐ AND PROCEED TO QUESTION 22 IN PART III

18. To what extent do budget policies and procedures vary across profit centers in your company?

   a. Budgets are not used at the profit center level   4

   b. No variation across profit centers 113

   c. Slight variation across profit centers 111

   d. Moderate variation across profit centers 57

   e. Considerable variation across profit centers 18

   f. Each profit center has its own policies & procedures . 15

19. Do you have managers or groups with the following title or equivalent in a typical profit center of your company?

Title	Presence of manager/group	
	Yes	No
a. Controller	244	76
b. Budget Manager	134	165
c. Long-range Planning Committee	53	240
d. Budget Committee	36	253
e. Internal Audit Manager	73	219
f. Planning Manager	119	182
g. Industrial Engineer	135	169
h. Standards Department	94	201

20. Do your profit centers use computers for budget-related purposes?

☐ Yes 273   ☐ No 40

If yes,

   a. Do profit centers have direct access to their profit center's data base? 222 Yes   63 No

   b. Do corporate managers have direct access to the data bases of various profit centers? 114 Yes   170 No

   c. Where are budget performance reports of profit centers prepared? (Check one box.)
   133 Corporate Office 143 Profit Center 8 Not prepared

   d. Are the computers at the corporate and the profit center levels compatible with each other? 211 Yes 61   No

21. Listed below are several "organizational devices" that are frequently used for managing relationships between corporate headquarters and profit centers. We would like to know the relative importance corporate top management places on these devices in managing corporate profit center relationships.

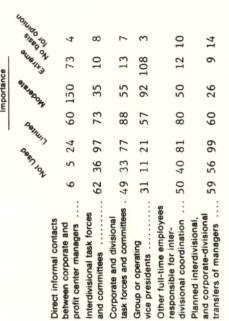
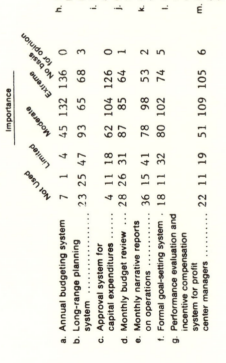

	Not Used	Importance				Extreme	No basis for opinion
		Limited	Moderate				
a. Annual budgeting system	7	1	4	45	132	136	0
b. Long-range planning system	23	25	47	93	65	68	3
c. Approval system for capital expenditures	4	11	18	62	104	126	0
d. Monthly budget review	28	26	31	87	85	64	1
e. Monthly narrative reports on operations	36	15	41	78	98	53	2
f. Formal goal-setting system	18	11	32	80	102	74	5
g. Performance evaluation and incentive compensation system for profit center managers	22	11	19	51	109	105	6
h. Direct informal contacts between corporate and profit center managers	6	5	24	60	150	73	4
i. Interdivisional task forces and committees	62	36	97	73	35	10	8
j. Corporate and divisional task forces and committees	49	33	77	88	55	13	7
k. Group or operating vice presidents	31	11	21	57	92	108	3
l. Other full-time employees responsible for interdivisional coordination	50	40	81	80	50	12	10
m. Planned interdivisional, and corporate-divisional transfers of managers	59	56	99	60	26	9	14

PART III: LONG-RANGE PLANNING

22. Indicate the general areas in which your company makes formalized plans or budgets? (Circle one number in each row.)

	Not Used	1 year or less	2 to 3 years	4 to 5 years	over 5 years
			Plan or Budget Period		
a. Profits	6	131	79	147	27
b. Sales	8	133	74	142	33
b. Expenses	4	156	75	128	24
c. Production targets	85	133	48	80	22
e. Capital expenditures	10	139	83	123	33
f. Market share	115	85	48	101	21
g. Return on capital	68	92	63	134	30
h. Number of employees	55	164	56	92	13
i. Other (Specify.) _____	19	8	7	16	4

IF YOU DO NOT USE LONG-RANGE PLANS (PLAN PERIOD 2 OR MORE YEARS) FOR ANY OF THE ABOVE AREAS, PLEASE PROCEED TO QUESTION 27 IN PART IV.

---

23. (a) How frequently do you update your long-range plans? (Check one box.)

279 Annually   5 Once in 5 years

12 Once in 3 years   35 As needed

(b) How many months before the end of fiscal period do you:

Commence the formal long-range planning process _____

Complete the formal long-range planning process _____

(c) What is the title of the person primarily responsible for developing the long-range plan for the company as a whole?

_____

SEE EXHIBIT I

24. (a) Usually, how tight is the linkage between the numbers used in the first year of your long-range plan and the corresponding year's annual budget?

123 Identical   101 Slightly different

80 Almost the same   24 Very different

(b) What proportion of managers participating in the preparation of long-range plans are also involved in developing budgets?

☐ None ☐ Some ☐ Many ☐ Most ☐ No basis for opinion
6   82   58   182   3

25. (a) Are your long-term plans broken up into medium-term or short-term programs or projects?

☐ Yes   ☐ No
186   142

(b) If YES, are project approvals made prior to the commencement of the budget cycles?

☐ Yes   ☐ No
122   73

IF YOUR COMPANY IS NOT DIVIDED INTO PROFIT CENTERS, PLEASE PROCEED TO QUESTION 27 IN PART IV.

---

26. What proportion of your profit centers prepare long-range plans?

☐ None ☐ Some ☐ Many ☐ Most ☐ All
24   35   6   44   171

PART IV: BUDGETING

27. Indicate below the types of forecasts which are developed in your company before preparing the budget.

		Period covered by forecast		
	Not Used	Quart.	Semi-Annual	Annual
a. General economic conditions ..	69	66	15	226
b. Sales estimates for industry	133	43	11	176
c. Your company's market share ..	145	42	10	166
d. Sales estimate	38	104	16	220
for your company	17	10	2	20
e. Others (Specify.)				

28. (a) What are the principal procedures used in making your sales forecasts either for long-range planning or budgeting? (Check applicable boxes.)

	Long-range Plan			Annual Budget		
	not used	used occasionally	used frequently	not used	used occasionally	used frequently
1. Analysis of historical data ..	16	66	248	4	55	321
2. Opinions of company mgrs. .	20	64	243	6	54	317
3. Industry analysis	48	110	166	58	134	173
3. Outside consultants	199	103	22	158	72	21
5. Economic Models	125	121	81	150	125	84
6. Other (Specify.)						
────────────────────	18	2	12	15	2	12

(b) Which of the above procedures do you emphasize most while preparing:

Long Range Plan _____ Annual Budget _____

29. (a) Do you use the following techniques for scheduling and monitoring the preparation of budgets?

	yes	no
1. Gantt Charts	46	309
2. Critical path method	78	283
3. Program evaluation and review technique (PERT)	64	294
4. Other (Specify.)	41	49

(b) How many months before the end of fiscal period do you:

Commence the formal budgetary process _____ months
Complete the formal budgetary process __ __ months

(c) When does your fiscal year begin? _____calendar month

Jan.	256	April	4	July	15	Oct.	49
Feb.	17	May	3	Aug.	4	Nov.	12
March	4	June	5	Sept.	13	Dec.	8

30. (a) Do you have a budget manual or its equivalent?

      ☐ Yes   ☐ No
      253   140

(b) Do you use preprinted budget forms?

      ☐ Yes   ☐ No
      349   43

(c) Do you have a formal procedure for evaluating the extent to which budgets are being prepared and used effectively by your managers?

      ☐ Yes   ☐ No
      147   241

If YES, please describe briefly the procedure used and the title of the manager who is in charge of such an evaluation.

Procedure used: _____

SEE EXHIBIT II
_____

Title of evaluating manager: _____

SEE EXHIBIT I
_____

31. Please circle the number which best indicates the relative proportion of the work involved in budgeting activities for which detailed, comprehensive procedures are used in your company. (Circle one number.)

Few established rules and procedures			Detailed rules and procedures		
0%	20%	40%	60%	80%	100%
3	41	81	108	117	26

32. What proportion of your control reports covering the current performance of a manager are matched with his or her organizational authority and responsibility? (Check one number.)

☐ None	☐ Some	☐ Many	☐ Most	☐ All
30	79	59	145	68

33. Check the items below which are used as a standard (or yardstick) in your company to measure, control, and/or evaluate current sales or service revenues. (Check all used.)

☐ Historical revenue data 278   ☐ Sales quotas 81

☐ Sales forecasts 255   ☐ Other ___24___

☐ Sales budgets 289   ☐ None of the above 13

34. (a) Check the items below which are used as a standard (or yard-stick) in your company to measure, control, and/or evaluate actual costs and expenses. (Check all used.)

☐ Use historical costs 316
☐ Labor standards 181
☐ Materials standards 135
☐ Standard costs 171
☐ Cost ratios 196
☐ Direct/variable costs 160
☐ Expense/cost budgets for materials 196
☐ Expense/cost budgets for overhead 227
☐ Expense/cost budgets for labor 246
☐ Budgets for selling expenses 254
☐ Budgets for overhead expenses 288
☐ Other _____ 18

(b) Usually do you use flexible budgets while preparing performance reports based on the above standards?

☐ Yes 106 ☐ No 279

(c) Do you usually classify expenses into controllable and non-controllable categories while preparing performance reports?

☐ Yes 210 ☐ No 181

35. How does your company convey to each manager or supervisor a clear understanding of the responsibilities of his department or profit center included in the Plan of Operations or Budget? (Check all appropriate boxes.)

Responsibilities are communicated by	To		
	Senior Mgrs	Middle Mgt	Supervisors or Foremen
a. Formal conferences	284	136	50
b. Informal conferences	128	224	164
c. Copy of the operating plan	251	199	78
d. Other (Specify.) _____	13	14	15

36. (a) What period of time does your budget cover, and how is it broken down by interim periods? (Circle one number.)

Multi-year, broken down by years/quarters 15
Annually, broken down by months 308
Annually, broken down by quarters 44
Quarterly, broken down by months 4
Semi-annually, broken down by months 11
Other (Specify.) ————————————————— 11

(b) Do you usually prepare:

1. Contingency plans/budgets   130 Yes   257 No
2. Rolling budgets   77 Yes   293 No

37. Do you subdivide your budget by the following categories?

a. By product lines   226 Yes 150 No
b. By major subunits of the company   357 Yes   30 No

38. Is a separate report comparing actual current performance with standards of performance or budget objectives prepared for each department or profit center (or its equivalent)?

378 Yes   14 No

If YES, check below the type of report indicating the frequency of preparation.

	Frequency of preparation			
	Daily	Weekly	Monthly	Quarterly
a. Sales	34	29	272	14
b. Profits	26	310	7	1
c. Costs	18	336	9	2
d. General administrative expenses	50	21	329	2
e. Distribution expenses	114	19	267	2
f. Factory overhead (burden)	174	15	210	3
g. Other (Specify.)	5	17	4	2

39. Where a report shows a significant deviation from the company's standards of performance or budget, how is it generally handled? (Check all applicable.)

261 ☐ Written explanation of the causes of such deviation?

170 ☐ An indication of corrective action taken?

217 ☐ A discussion of the deviation with immediate supervisor?

152 ☐ An oral explanation?

19 ☐ Other (Specify.) _____

_____

_____

40. When did your company last make a significant change in its budgetary policies, procedures, or practices?

☐ less than one year ago   103

☐ 1 to 3 years ago 119

☐ more than three years ago   164

If your company made significant changes during the past three years, briefly describe the nature of the change.

_____

_____

_____

41. In the past year, how frequently do you think that the managers in your company engaged in the following behaviors in order to comply with budgetary controls? (Circle one number in each row.)

	never	rarely	some-times	frequ-ently	almost always
a. Employed contract labor to get needed work done, while staying within headcount limits ...	88	123	138	29	4
b. Got required approvals after money was spent in order to speed up the process	36	182	145	19	1
c. Bought equipment from outside the company, so that the design portion of the expenditure could be capitalized, even though it could have been designed within the company	183	142	38	4	0
d. Shifted funds between accounts to avoid budget overruns	91	127	127	34	4
e. Pulled profits from future period: (i) deferring needed expenditure	72	105	164	38	2
(ii) accelerating a sale	132	113	102	21	2
(iii) accelerated a capital expenditure or other expenses because funds were available in the budget for the period	70	136	143	29	0
f. Other (Specify.) ————	5	0	2	1	1

42. All in all, how would you rate the effectiveness of your budgetary process in facilitating the accomplishment of your company's objectives? (Circle one number.)

Ineffective	2
Poor	13
Neither poor nor good	70
Good 255
Extremely effective	53

PART V: BUDGET MANAGER

This part deals only with the person primarily responsible for the financial expression of the combined objectives and goals of various organizational units in the form of a coordinated plan of operations or budgets for the top management. If the person completing the questionnaire does not hold the above responsibility, he or she should not complete this part.

43. (a) Title: _____ SEE EXHIBIT I _____

Reports to: _____ SEE EXHIBIT I _____

(b) When was this position established? _____ calendar year

(c) Educational background: (Check all applicable.) SEE EXHIBIT III

☐ Junior college or less

☐ Undergraduate degree in _____

☐ Graduate degree in _____

☐ Professional certification in _____

(d) Work Experience:

1. Years in the current job _____
2. Years with the current employer _____
3. Years in current or closely related industries _____
4. Years of experience in accounting/finance _____
5. Years of experience in non-financial areas (Specify.) _____

_____

44. What are the major goals on which your performance is evaluated?

a. _____

b. _____

c. _____

d. _____

45. What proportion of your time is spent in the following activities?

Coordinating and preparing the budget	_____ %
Monitoring performance against budget	_____ %
Followup and corrective action	_____ %
TOTAL	100%

**THANK YOU FOR PARTICIPATING IN THIS RESEARCH.
YOUR RESPONSES WILL BE TREATED AS STRICTLY CONFIDENTIAL.
WE WILL GLADLY SEND YOU A SUMMARY
OF THE SURVEY RESULTS.**

NAME OF THE PERSON COMPLETING THE QUESTIONNAIRE

_____

_____

TITLE _____

NAME OF ORGANIZATION _____

ADDRESS _____

_____

PHONE _____

MAY WE LIST THE NAME OF YOUR COMPANY AS A PARTICIPANT IN
THIS RESEARCH (ALTHOUGH WE WILL NOT DISCLOSE YOUR
SPECIFIC RESPONSE)?
286 ☐ YES   107 ☐ NO

Please mail completed questionnaire to:
**Professor Srinivasan Umapathy
Boston University School of Management
704 Commonwealth Avenue
Boston, MA 02215**

Exhibit I
Title of Managers Responsible for Specific Activities

Titles	23C Long Range Plan (%)	30C Budget Evaluation (%)	43A(Title) Corporate Financial Planner (%)	43A(Reports to) Corporate Financial Planner (%)
		Question Numbers		
Chairman of the Board				
Chairman				
Chief Executive Officer	7.5	6.6	.3	4.9
President				
Chief Operating Officer	11.3	8.1	.7	9.1
Executive Fice President	6.0	4.4	2.4	2.8
Vice President Finance				
Chief Financial Officer	12.0	11.0	10.1	23.4
V.P. Planning				
Director of Planning				
Budget Director				
Treasurer	46.9	29.4	55.8	15.0
Manager of Planning				
Director Corporate Development				

Exhibit I—*Continued*

| Titles | Question Numbers | | | |
	23C Long Range Plan (%)	30C Budget Evaluation (%)	43A(Title) Corporate Financial Planner (%)	43A(Reports to) Corporate Financial Planner (%)
Assistant Director of Planning Assistant V.P. Planning	0.9	1.5	3.5	0.4
Corporate Controller	4.7	12.5	13.6	31.1
Assistant Controller	0.9	1.5	6.3	7.0
V.P. Corporate Development	1.6	1.5	–	0.4
Other	8.2	23.5	7.3	5.9
Total	100.0	100.0	100.0	100.0

Exhibit II
Procedures Used to Evaluate Effective Preparation
and Use of Budgets (Question 30-C)

Procedures	Percentages
Monthly Evaluation	13.9
Monthly Budget vs. Actual Comparison	6.5
Compare Actual to Planned	17.4
Variance Reports	13.8
Other Numbers Oriented Procedure	9.4
Formal Reviews	15.9
Informal Discussions	5.8
Business Review Meetings	3.6
Monthly Review of Managers	2.9
Operational Reviews	4.3
CED Reviews	0.7
Business Plan Reviews	-
Responsibility Reporting	0.7
Other	5.1
Total	100.0

Exhibit III
Educational Background of the Corporate Budget Manager
(Question 43-C)

Education	Percentages
Junior College or less	1.4
Junior College or less + Professional Certification	-
Undergraduate degree in Accounting	16.9
Undergraduation to degree in Accounting + Professional Certification	8.5
Undergraduate degree in Non-Accounting	9.2
Undergraduate degree in Non-Accounting + Professional Certification	3.5
MBA	29.2
MBA + Professional Certification	9.5
Graduate Degree other than MBA	15.1
Graduate Degree other than MBA + Professional Certification	6.7
Total	100.0

Appendix II

A Partial List of Participating Firms

The following firms authorized us to identify them as participants in this study. The firms are listed alphabetically by industry in the following order—Commercial Banks, Diversified Finance, Diversified Service, Hospitals, Life Insurance, Manufacturing: Large Firms, Manufacturing: Medium-sized Companies, Retail/Wholesale Trade, Transportation, and Utilities.

COMMERCIAL BANKS (Total Responses = 50)

1. Am South Bank Corporation
2. Arizona Bank
3. Atlantic National Bank of Florida
4. Bank Leumi Trust Co.
5. Bank of New England Corporation
6. Bank of Oklahoma, NA
7. Bank of Virginia Corporation
8. Barnett Banks of Florida, Inc.
9. Bay Banks, Inc.
10. Centerre Bancorp.
11. Central Fidelity Bank

12. Central Trust Co.
13. Citicorp
14. Citizens and Southern Georgia Corporation
15. Continental Illinois Corporation
16. Core States Financial Corporation
17. Deposit Guaranty National Bank
18. Dominion Bankshares Corporation
19. Fifth Third Bank
20. First Atlanta Corporation
21. First of America Bank Corporation
22. First National State Bancorp
23. First City Bancorp of Texas
24. First Union Corporation
25. Hibernia National Bank in New Orleans
26. Idaho First National Bank
27. Industry Valley Bank and Trust Co.
28. Interfirst Bank Austin
29. LaSalle National Bank
30. Mellon National Corporation
31. Mercantile Texas Corporation
32. National Westminister Bank, USA
33. Puget Sound National Bank
34. J. Henry Schroder Bank and Trust Co.
35. San Diego Trust and Savings Bank
36. Souran Financial Corporation
37. South Carolina National Bank
38. Suburban Bank
39. Texas Commerce Bancshares, Inc.
40. United States Trust of New York
41. Wachovia Corporation
42. Wilmington Trust Co.

DIVERSIFIED FINANCE (Total Responses = 15)

1. American Express Company
2. American Family Corporation
3. American General Companies
4. CIGNA Corporation
5. The Chubb Corporation
6. City Federal Savings and Loans Association
7. Colonial Penn Group, Inc.
8. Federal National Mortgage Association

9. Frank B. Hall & Co., Inc.
10. Fremont General Corporation
11. Lincoln National Corporation
12. Marsh and McLennan Companies
13. The Travelers Corporation
14. U.S. Leasing International, Inc.

DIVERSIFIED SERVICE (Total Responses = 22)

1. American Hospital Supply Corporation
2. Amfac Inc.
3. Associated Milk Producers, Inc.
4. Browning-Ferris Industries, Inc.
5. Fluor Corporation
6. Hilton Hotels Corporation
7. Landmark, Inc.
8. Pioneer Hi-Bred International, Inc.
9. Rollins, Inc.
10. Tesoro Petroleum Corporation
11. Suburban Propane Gas Corporation
12. Sunkist Growers, Inc.
13. Super Food Services, Inc.
14. Walt Disney Productions
15. Whittaker Corporation

HOSPITALS (Total Responses = 36)

1. Addison Gilbert Hospital
2. Berkshire Medical Center
3. Beverly Hospital
4. Brigham and Women's Hospital
5. Brockton Hospital
6. Cape Cod Hospital
7. Carney Hospital
8. Choate Symmes Hospital
9. Faulkner Hospital
10. Franklin County Public Hospital
11. Harvard Community Health Plan Hospital
12. Holden District Hospital
13. Hubbard Regional Hospital
14. Lawrence General Hospital
15. Leominister Hospital

16. Leonard Morse Hospital
17. Lowell General Hospital
18. Mary Lane Hospital
19. Massachusetts General Hospital
20. Melrose-Wakefield Hospital
21. Mount Auburn Hospital
22. Nashoba Community Hospital
23. New England Deaconess Hospital
24. Saint Luke's Hospital
25. Santa Maria Hospital
26. Somerville Hospital
27. South Shore Hospital
28. University Hospital
29. Worcester Memorial Hospital, Inc.

LIFE INSURANCE (Total Responses = 26)

1. American United Life Insurance Co.
2. Bankers Life and Casualty Co.
3. Charter Security Life Insurance Co.
4. CNA Financial Corp.
5. Equitable Life Assurance Society of the U.S.
6. General American Life Insurance Co.
7. Home Life Insurance Company of New York
8. Kemper Investors Life
9. Massachusetts Mutual Life Insurance Co.
10. Metropolitan Life Insurance Co.
11. Mutual Life Insurance Company of New York
12. Northwestern National Life Insurance Co.
13. Phoenix Mutual Life Insurance Corp.
14. State Mutual Life Assurance Co.
15. Transamerica Occidental Life Insurance Co.
16. Union Mutual Life Insurance Co.

MANUFACTURING: LARGE FIRMS (Total Responses = 108)

1. Air Products and Chemicals, Inc.
2. AM International
3. American Cyanamid Co.
4. American Petrofina, Inc.
5. American Hoechst Corp.
6. Anderson Clayton & Co.

7. Anheuser Busch Co., Inc.
8. Becton Dickinson & Co.
9. Boise Cascade Corporation
10. C.F. Industries, Inc.
11. Campbell Soup Co.
12. Caterpillar Tractor Co.
13. Certain Teed Corporation
14. Continental Group, Inc.
15. Cooper Tire and Rubber Company
16. CPC International, Inc.
17. Crown Central Petroleum Corp.
18. Cummins Engine Co., Inc.
19. Easco Corporation
20. Ex-Cell-Corporation
21. Ferro Corporation
22. Fieldcrest Mills Ltd.
23. Figgie International, Inc.
24. FMC Corporation
25. Fuqua Industries, Inc.
26. General Electric Co.
27. General Mills, Inc.
28. Gifford-Hill & Co., Inc.
29. Gulf Oil
30. Harnischfeger Corporation
31. Hercules, Inc.
32. Hewlett-Packard Co.
33. Honeywell, Inc.
34. Hoover Universal, Inc.
35. James River Corporation of Virginia
36. Jim Walter Corporation
37. Johnson and Johnson Co.
38. Johnson Controls, Inc.
39. Thomas J. Lipton, Inc.
40. Manville Corporation
41. MAPCO, Inc.
42. McCormick & Co., Inc.
43. Media General, Inc.
44. Mobay Chemical Corporation
45. Monsanto Co.
46. Morton-Thiokol Products, Inc.
47. National Cooperative Refinery Association
48. National Intergroup, Inc.

49. National Semiconductor Corporation
50. NCR Corporation
51. North American Coal Corporation
52. Owens-Corning Fiberglas Corp.
53. Pabst Brewing
54. Parker-Hannifin Corp.
55. Phillips Petroleum
56. Pillsbury Co.
57. Quaker State Oil Refining Corporation
58. Ralston-Purina Co.
59. Raychem Corporation
60. Rexnord, Inc.
61. R.J. Reynolds Industries
62. Royal Crown Companies, Inc.
63. Sanders Associates Inc.
64. Scovill, Inc.
65. Joseph E. Seagram & Sons, Inc.
66. Smith Kline Beckman Corp.
67. A.O. Smith Corporation
68. Sonoco Products Co.
69. A.E. Staley Manufacturing Co.
70. Stanley Works
71. Storage Technology Corporation
72. Swift Independent Packing Company
73. Tribune Co.
74. Union Pacific Corporation
75. U.S. Gypsum Co.
76. Warnaco, Inc.
77. Warner-Lambert Co.
78. Westinghouse Electric Corporation
79. Zenith Radio Corporation

MANUFACTURING: MEDIUM-SIZED COMPANIES
(Total Responses = 42)

1. Accu Ray Corporation
2. Adams Russell Co., Inc.
3. AEL Industries, Inc.
4. Aeroquip Corporation
5. American Microsystems, Inc.
6. Ametek, Inc.
7. Analog Devices, Inc.
8. Applied Materials, Inc.

9. Applied Digital Data Systems, Inc.
10. Atlantic Research Corporation
11. Avantek Inc.
12. Barber-Coleman Co.
13. Cincinnati Electronics Corporation
14. Clevepak Corporation
15. Contraves-Goerz Corporation
16. Craig Corporation
17. CTS Corporation
18. Elcor Corporation
19. Esterline Corporation
20. Giddings and Lewis, Inc.
21. Gleason Works
22. Huck Manufacturing Co.
23. IMC Magnetics Corporation
24. Kirkwood Industries, Inc.
25. Sealed Power Corporation
26. Valley Steel Products Co.

RETAIL/WHOLESALE TRADE (Total Responses = 29)

1. Albertson's Inc.
2. Ames Department Stores, Inc.
3. J.L. Brandeis Department Stores
4. Chatham Supermarkets, Inc.
5. Fisher's Big Wheel, Inc.
6. Giant Food, Inc.
7. Goldblatt Brothers, Inc.
8. Higbee Co.
9. Household International, Inc.
10. The May Department Stores Co.
11. Marriott Corporation
12. McDonald's Corporation
13. The Southland Corporation
14. U.S. Shoe Corporation
15. Walgreen Co.
16. Woodward and Lothrap, Inc.
17. Zayre Corporation

TRANSPORTATION (Total Responses = 17)

1. Alexander and Baldwin, Inc.
2. ARCO Pipeline

3. Bekins Company
4. Burlington Northern, Inc.
5. CSX Corporation
6. Emery Air Freight Corporation
7. Norfolk Southern Corporation
8. Pan American World Airways, Inc.
9. Piedmont Aviation, Inc.
10. Tidewater, Inc.
11. Trans World Corporation

UTILITIES (Total Responses = 28)

1. American Electric Power Co. Inc.
2. American Natural Resources Co.
3. American Telephone and Telegraph Co.
4. Arizona Public Service Co.
5. Baltimore Gas and Electric Co.
6. Columbia Gas System, Inc.
7. Commonwealth Edison Co.
8. Consolidated Edison of New York, Inc.
9. Consolidated Natural Gas Co.
10. Florida Power and Light Co.
11. GPU Service Corporation
12. GTE Corporation
13. Gulf States Utilities Co.
14. Internorth, Inc.
15. Middle South Utilities, Inc.
16. Niagara Mohawk Power Corp.
17. Northeast Utilities
18. Northern Indiana Public Service Co.
19. Pacific Gas and Electric Co.
20. Pennsylvania Power and Light Co.
21. Public Service Electric and Gas Co.
22. Sonat, Inc.
23. Southern California Edison Co.
24. Texas Utilities Co.
25. Transco Energy Co.
26. Virginia Electric and Power Co.

Bibliography

Ansari, Shahid. "An Integrated Approach to Control System Design," *Accounting, Organizations and Society*, 1977, pp. 101-112.

————. "Toward an Open Systems to Approach Budgeting," *Accounting, Organizations and Society*, 1979, pp. 149-161.

Anthony, Robert N. *Planning and Control Systems: A Framework for Analysis*. Cambridge: Division of Research, Harvard Business School, 1965.

————. "Management Accounting for the Future," *Sloan Management Review*, Spring 1972, pp. 17-31.

Anthony, Robert N., and John Dearden, *Management Control Systems*. Homewood, Ill.: Richard D. Irwin, Inc., 1980.

Argyris, Chris. *The Impact of Budgets on People*. Controllership Foundation, 1952.

Barnard, C. I. *The Functions of the Executive*. Cambridge: Harvard University Press, 1938.

Bass, B. M., and H. J. Leavitt. "Some Experiments in Planning and Operating," *Management Science*, July 1963, pp. 574-585.

Becker, S., and D. Green, Jr. "Budgeting and Employee Behavior," *Journal of Business*, October 1962, pp. 392-402.

Bonini, C. P. *Simulation of Information and Decision Systems in the Firm*. Englewood Cliffs, N.J.: Prentice-Hall, Inc., 1963.

Brownell, Peter. "Participation in Budgeting, Locus of Control and Organizational Effectiveness," *The Accounting Review,* October 1981, pp. 844-860.

_____. "The Motivational Impact of Management-By-Exception in a Budgetary Context," *Journal of Accounting Research,* Autumn 1983, pp. 456-472.

Brownell, Peter, and Morris McInnes. "Budgetary Participation, Motivation, and Managerial Performance," *The Accounting Review,* October 1986, pp. 587-600.

Bruere, H., and A. Lazarus. *Applied Budgeting.* New York: A. W. Shaw Company, 1926.

Brummet, R. L., W. C. Pyle, and E. G. Flamholtz, "Human Resource Measurement—A Challenge for Accountants," *The Accounting Review,* 1968, pp. 217-224.

Bruns, William J. "Accounting Information and Decision Making: Some Behavioral Hypotheses," *The Accounting Review,* July 1968, pp. 469-480.

Bruns, William J., and J. H. Waterhouse. "Budgetary Control and Organization Structure," *Journal of Accounting Research,* Autumn 1975, pp. 177-203.

Bryan, J. F., and E. A. Locke. "Goal Setting as a Means of Increasing Motivation," *Journal of Applied Psychology,* June 1967, pp. 274-277.

Burns, Thomas J. *The Behavioral Aspects of Accounting Data for Performance Evaluation.* Columbus: Ohio State University College of Administrative Science, 1969.

Cammann, C. "Effects of the Use of Control Systems," *Accounting, Organizations and Society,* 1976, pp. 301-313.

Carroll, S. J., and H. L. Tosi. "Goal Characteristics and Personality Factors in a Management by Objectives Program," *Administrative Science Quarterly,* September 1970, pp. 295-305.

Cherrington, D. J., and J. O. Cherrington. "Appropriate Reinforcement Contingencies in the Budgeting Process, Empirical Research in Accounting: Selected Studies, 1973." *Supplement to Journal of Accounting Research,* pp. 225-253.

Collins, B. E., and H. Guetzkow. *A Social Psychology of Group Processes for Decision Making.* New York: Wiley, 1964.

Collins, Frank. "The Interaction of Budget Characteristics and Personality Variables with Budgetary Response Attitudes," *The Accounting Review,* April 1978, pp. 324-335.

Dearborn, D. C., and H. A. Simon, "Selective Perception: A Note on the Departmental Identifications of Executives," *Sociometry,* June 1958.

De Coster, D. T., and J. P. Fertakis. "Budget-Induced Pressure and Its

Relationship to Supervisory Behavior," *Journal of Accounting Research,* Autumn 1968, pp. 237-246.

Dillard, J. F., and J. Jiambalvo. "Expectancy Theory in a Budgeting Setting: A Comment," *The Accounting Review,* July 1979, pp. 630-634.

Dunbar, R. L. M. "Budgeting for Control," *Administrative Science Quarterly,* March 1971, pp. 88-96.

Etzioni, A. *Complex Organizations.* New York: Holt, Rinehart and Winston, 1961.

Foran, M. F., and D. De Coster. "An Experimental Study of the Effects of Participation, Authoritarianism, and Feedback on Cognitive Dissonance in a Standard Setting Situation," *The Accounting Review,* October 1974, pp. 751-763.

French, J. R. P., E. Kay, and H. H. Meyer, "Participation and the Appraisal System," *Human Relations,* February 1966, pp. 3-20.

Henderson, B. D., and J. Dearden. "New System for Divisional Control," *Harvard Business Review,* September-October 1966, pp. 144-160.

Hofstede, Geert H. *The Game of Budget Control.* Van Gorcum, 1967.

Hopwood, Anthony G. "An Empirical Study of the Role of Accounting Data in Performance Evaluation," Empirical Research in Accounting: Selected Studies, 1972, *Supplement to Journal of Accounting Research,* pp. 156-182.

_____. *Accounting and Human Behavior.* Milwaukee, Wisc.: Haymarket Publishing Limited, 1974.

_____. "Towards an Organizational Perspective for the Study of Accounting and Information Systems," *Accounting, Organizations and Society,* 1978, pp. 3-13.

Horngren, Charles T. *Cost Accounting: A Managerial Emphasis.* 6th ed. Englewood Cliffs, N.J.: Prentice-Hall, 1982.

Jasinski, F. J. "Use and Misuse of Efficiency Controls," *Harvard Business Review,* July-August, 1956, pp. 105-112.

Johnson, G. G. *The Role of Formal Evaluation in the Process of Budgetary Control.* Unpublished Dissertation. Harvard Business School, 1972.

Kenis, I. "Effects of Budgetary Goal Characteristics on Managerial Attitudes and Performace," *The Accounting Review,* October 1979, pp. 707-721.

Lawler, Edward E. *Motivation in Work Organizations.* Monterey, Calif.: Brooks/Cole, 1973.

Lawler, Edward E., and John G. Rhode. *Information and Control in Organizations.* Goodyear Publishing Co., Inc., 1976.

Lowe, E. A., and R. A. Shaw. "An Analysis of Managerial Biasing: Evidence from a Company's Budgeting Process," *The Journal of*

Management Studies, 1968, pp. 304-315.

_____. "The Accuracy of Short-Term Business Forecasting: An Analysis of a Firm's Sales Budgeting," *The Journal of Industrial Economics,* 1970, pp. 275-289.

Maier, N. R. F. *Problem Solving Discussions and Conferences: Leadership Methods and Skills.* New York: McGraw-Hill, 1963.

Maslow, A. H. *Motivation and Personality.* New York: Harper and Row, 1954.

Mautz, R. K., W. G. Kell, A. G. Merten, R. R. Reilly, D. G. Severence, and B. J. White. *Internal Control in U.S. Corporations: The State of the Art.* Morristown, N.J.: Financial Executives Research Foundation, 1980.

Merchant, Kenneth A. "The Design of the Corporate Budgeting System: Influences on Managerial Behavior and Performance," *The Accounting Review,* October 1981, pp. 813-829.

Milani, K. "The Relationship of Participation in Budget Setting to Industrial Supervisor Performance and Attitudes: A Field Study," *The Accounting Review,* April 1975, pp. 274-284.

Onsi, M. "Factor Analysis of Behavioral Variables Affecting Budgetary Slack," *The Accounting Review,* July 1973, pp. 535-548.

Ridgway, V. F. "Dysfunctional Consequences of Performance Measurements," *Administrative Science Quarterly,* September 1956, pp. 240-247.

Rockness, H. O. "Expectancy Theory in a Budgeting Setting: An Examination," *The Accounting Review,* October 1977, pp. 893-903.

Roethlisberger, F. J., and W. J. Dickson. *Management and the Worker.* Cambridge: Harvard University Press, 1939.

Ronen, J., and J. L. Livingstone, "An Expectancy Theory Approach to the Motivational Impact of Budgets," *The Accounting Review,* October 1975, pp. 671-685.

Rosen, L. S., and R. A. Schenck, "Some Behavioral Consequences of Accounting Measurement Systems," *Cost and Management,* October 1967, pp. 6-16.

San Miguel, J. G. "The Behavioral Sciences and Concepts and Standards for Management Planning and Control," *Accounting, Organizations and Society,* 1977, pp. 177-186.

Schiff, M., and A. Y. Lewin. "Where Traditional Budgeting Fails," *The Accounting Review,* May 1968, pp. 50-62.

_____. "The Impact of People on Budgets," *The Accounting Review,* April 1970, pp. 259-268.

Searfoss, D. G. "Some Behavioral Aspects of Budgeting for Control: An Empirical Study," *Accounting, Organizations and Society,* 1976, pp. 375-385.

Sord, B. H., and G. A. Welsch. *Business Budgeting.* Controllership Foundation, 1958.

Stedry, A. C. *Budget Control and Cost Behavior.* Englewood Cliffs, N.J.: Prentice-Hall, 1960.

Stedry, A. C., and E. Kay. "The Effects of Goal Difficulty on Performance: A Field Experiment," *Behavioral Science,* November 1966, pp. 459-470.

Swieringa, R. J., and R. H. Moncur. *Some Effects of Participative Budgeting on Managerial Behavior.* Montvale, N.J.: National Association of Accountants, 1975.

Umapathy, S. "How Successful Firms Budget," *Management Accounting,* February 1987.

_____. "Unfavorable Variances in Budgeting," in Ferris, K. R., and J. L. Livingstone, eds., *Managerial Accounting: The Behavioral Foundations.* Rev. Ed. Beavercreek, Ohio: Century VII Publishing Co., 1987.

Welsch, G. A. *Budgeting: Profit Planning and Control.* 4th ed. Englewood Cliffs, N.J.: Prentice-Hall, 1976.

Index